CW01369536

NEURODIVERGENT, BY NATURE

NEURODIVERGENT, BY NATURE
Why Biodiversity Needs Neurodiversity

Joe Harkness

BLOOMSBURY WILDLIFE
LONDON · OXFORD · NEW YORK · NEW DELHI · SYDNEY

BLOOMSBURY WILDLIFE
Bloomsbury Publishing Plc
50 Bedford Square, London, WC1B 3DP, UK
Bloomsbury Publishing Ireland Limited,
29 Earlsfort Terrace, Dublin 2, D02 AY28, Ireland

BLOOMSBURY, BLOOMSBURY WILDLIFE and the Diana logo are trademarks of
Bloomsbury Publishing Plc

First published in the United Kingdom 2025

Copyright © Joe Harkness, 2025

Joe Harkness has asserted his right under the Copyright, Designs and Patents Act, 1988,
to be identified as Author of this work.

For legal purposes the Acknowledgements on p. 247 constitute an extension of this
copyright page.

All rights reserved. No part of this publication may be: i) reproduced or transmitted in
any form, electronic or mechanical, including photocopying, recording or by means
of any information storage or retrieval system without prior permission in writing
from the publishers; or ii) used or reproduced in any way for the training, development
or operation of artificial intelligence (AI) technologies, including generative AI
technologies. The rights holders expressly reserve this publication from the text and
data mining exception as per Article 4(3) of the Digital Single Market Directive
(EU) 2019/790.

Bloomsbury Publishing Plc does not have any control over, or responsibility for, any
third-party websites referred to or in this book. All internet addresses given in this
book were correct at the time of going to press. The author and publisher regret any
inconvenience caused if addresses have changed or sites have ceased to exist, but can
accept no responsibility for any such changes.

A catalogue record for this book is available from the British Library

Library of Congress Cataloguing-in-Publication data has been applied for

ISBN: HB: 978-1-3994-1336-7; Audio: 978-1-3994-1339-8;
ePub: 978-1-3994-1337-4; ePDF: 978-1-3994-1338-1

2 4 6 8 10 9 7 5 3 1

Typeset in Bembo Std by Deanta Global Publishing Services, Chennai, India
Printed and bound in Great Britain by CPI Group (UK) Ltd, Croydon CR0 4YY

To find out more about our authors and books visit www.bloomsbury.com
and sign up for our newsletters.

For product safety related questions contact productsafety@bloomsbury.com.

Contents

Chapter One   7
No, you're macerating the moth abdomens!
– Introducing neurodiversity and nature

Chapter Two   25
Dia and Gignoskein – Seeking diagnosis

Chapter Three   43
Intolerable tyrants in the dock of the kangaroo
court – Experiences in education

Chapter Four   59
Hugging a tree for a dopamine fix
– The importance of nature

Chapter Five   77
More than just the saviour of the orangutan
– The conservation sector

Chapter Six   93
Out of the box and into the holographic forest
– Strengths

Chapter Seven   111
Cutting the toe pads off hundreds of dead parrots
– Achievements

Chapter Eight   129
Are you here to make the tea or take the notes?
– Barriers to access

Chapter Nine   145
Why is there a lump of multi-coloured playdough on my seat? – Reasonable adjustments

Chapter Ten   161
Peeking over the fence to see what next door are up to – Nature-related NGOs

Chapter Eleven   179
A rose-tinted perspective on the use of the infographic – Government agencies

Chapter Twelve   197
I think I'll eat my lunch in the bat chat corner today – Smaller conservation charities

Chapter Thirteen   213
Just give the naughtiest ones a sprig of lavender and a circular saw – Forest schools and care farms

Chapter Fourteen   231
Weaving words into golden threads – Why biodiversity needs neurodiversity

Acknowledgements   247
Further reading and resources   248
Index   251

CHAPTER ONE

No, you're macerating the moth abdomens!

Introducing neurodiversity and nature

'Ha, guess which three moth abdomens I put on to macerate an hour or so ago and am about to check their genitalia?'

In September 2021, these 23 words lit up my phone screen. To me, and anyone who has more than just a passing interest in moths, they made perfect sense. After all, it was I who put in the request for the maceration of the moth abdomens. So why did I keep looking at these words and laughing uncontrollably? I kept having to pause the washing-up to have another giggle about it, then wipe a stream of tears off each cheek using my bubble-laden forearms. Imagine if that message had been sent to the wrong person, or if someone else had read those words without any prior knowledge or context. What would they think? What do YOU think? Perhaps that I'm a member of some kind of bizarre moth fetish group? Whatever you're thinking, I hope you enjoy this little insight into the weird world of people with niche nature interests, and a contender for one of the funniest messages to appear in a naturalist's inbox. I'll tell you what I was thinking: how, has my interest in wildlife come to this?

Two months previously, I had caught two interesting moth species in our garden and had then come across another one in my grandparents' garden. I was confident with my identifications. I'm old-school, preferring to use reference books and photos, rather than an identification app. It takes away the fun and the challenge of working out what a species is. I was certain that all three were decent records for Norfolk, the county where I live. However, all three species required genitalia examination to confirm their identity before they could enter the lofty realms of the county moth recorder's sightings list. This process, known as 'gen. det.' involves the microscopic dissection and investigation of a range of insect genitalia, and at some point in the process, the use of a woodcock pin feather to stroke something or other. I'm not sure I really want to know what exactly. Why? Some clever cookie found out (again I don't want to know how) that both female and male moths have incredibly complex genitalia structures, like a fingerprint, which can be used to identify several species. There even exists a reference book for this, which I'm sure is a gripping page-turner. As far as nature niches go, this one is pretty specialist!

If you've no idea what moth trapping is, and have visions of me sadistically catching, torturing and murdering these timid butterflies of the night, I want to assure you that it's a humane activity. There are over 2,500 species of moth in the UK, split into two families, macro moths (the big ones) and micro moths (the tiny ones). This figure is likely to increase as climate change disperses moths into new areas. If you fancy learning more about the variety of the genus, you can invest in something known as a moth trap. It's basically a box with a light above it, as moths fly to light, although no one really knows why this is. Imagine an open receptacle, usually square or circular, with acrylic sheets angled down towards the middle, leaving an aperture for moths to fall in. You then stack empty egg cartons inside the box for the moths to crawl under and shelter, turn on the light above and leave it out overnight. In the morning, you go through the egg cartons and it's a bit like opening a present; you never know what's going to be in there.

Even the act of moth trapping, when put into words, comes across as a bit odd. This weirdness and that message about moths got me wondering about people interested in other niche wildlife topics. What drives someone to study the mating behaviour of garden spiders? And what corners does a person turn to lead them to a moment where they have to stroke the genitalia of a dead moth with a tiny feather? Pondering questions like these gave me an idea for a new book, and I quickly found myself engaging with a merry band of naturalists who focus on some fascinating niches, from woodlice to taxidermy. Then, after sharing my draft proposal with my now editor, I was thrown an almighty curveball. During an early conversation about my idea, they asked whether I knew anyone with niche nature-related interests who was neurodivergent (if you're unsure what this word means, don't worry). I shared that I'd quite recently discovered that I'm neurodivergent and said I wasn't sure if any of the naturalists I'd spoken to might also be neurodivergent. Now, of course, I wanted to find out.

It wasn't the biggest shock when most of the prospective contributors were candid enough to share that, yes, they are neurodivergent. Coincidental, perhaps, but I couldn't escape the bubbling feeling that lots of neurodivergent people might actually have a bit of an obsession with nature. I found myself wondering what drew them to it in the first place and if there's an intrinsic link between neurodivergence and wanting to work with the natural world. It was beginning to feel like I'd found a golden thread to run through the heart of the book. The whole idea couldn't have arisen at a more appropriate time, as I had recently been diagnosed with the condition known as attention deficit hyperactivity disorder, or ADHD for short. To paraphrase the National Health Service (NHS), ADHD is a behavioural condition that can make people seem restless, act impulsively and have difficulty concentrating. The symptoms are usually apparent in childhood, becoming more obvious at times when interactions with peers significantly increase, such as starting nursery or school. ADHD is also increasingly being diagnosed in adults, who, like me, recognise the symptoms, or someone else does.

No one truly knows what causes ADHD, but some research shows it can be more prevalent in people born prematurely, who had a low birthweight, or whose mothers used drugs, alcohol or tobacco during pregnancy, the first two of which apply to me. ADHD carries many labels. Some refer to it as a behavioural disorder, and some as a 'neurodevelopmental' disorder. A what, I hear you ask? First, I'd better introduce you to the DSM-5; not a *Star Wars* droid, rather the acronymic name for the Diagnostic and Statistical Manual (version 5), which is what medical professionals use to diagnose 'mental disorders'. The third version of the DSM was published in 1980, introducing 'developmental disorders', which then became known as 'neurodevelopmental disorders' in the DSM-5 when it was published in 2013. These are a group of conditions that manifest in the developmental period, which is loosely the time between birth and adulthood (0–18). These can cause impairment of personal, social, academic or occupational functioning. Although succinct, this is a rather general description for an incredibly complex range of issues, and the reality is that no list of impacts and symptoms will ever be fully representative of what 'real' people experience. Even differences present differently.

In the DSM-5, neurodevelopmental disorders diverge into six categories: intellectual disabilities, communication disorders, autism spectrum disorder, ADHD, specific learning disorder and motor disorders. These difficulties are often co-occurring, and you may also hear people use the terms 'comorbid' and 'dual diagnosis' to describe this, which means someone has been diagnosed with two or more conditions. Semantics start to get a bit messy at this point. 'Neurodevelopmental' is specific to the individual in question and concerns their own development and the level to which it enables them to function personally, socially, academically and occupationally. Two other terms, which both feel like recent additions to our vocabulary, have the neuro prefix: 'neurodiverse' and 'neurodivergent'. They describe the neurological differences evident across the entire population; the 'divergence' of neurodivergence is the difference itself, and the 'diversity' of neurodiversity is the whole range of differences. Neurodiversity includes neurotypical people, so it's a blanket term that includes everyone. To be neurodivergent is to identify oneself as different from societal norms. I hope this all makes sense to you, but don't worry if it doesn't. Read on, and you'll learn more.

Neurodivergent. It's in the title of the book, so let's focus on it. Both neurodiversity and neurodivergence are terms I use often in my work as a senior teacher in a complex needs school, but I didn't really consider myself as neurodivergent until recently. The first time was in the pitch for this book, trying to explain why I was the best person to write it. I said that being neurodivergent myself, with vast experience of working with neurodivergent young people, I felt able to approach this from a variety of angles. I suppose that through the initial planning and research process, reading and writing extensively about differences, I had become more comfortable with my own. There were reasons I'd been avoiding adding a label to myself, though. I felt cautious as I hadn't got a formal diagnosis of anything that fitted under that umbrella. I also felt (rightly or wrongly) that there would be significant stigma associated with identifying in this way, particularly in my job. I began recognising that although I felt knowledgeable on all things neurodivergence, not only was I repeatedly using the wrong terminology, but I also didn't fully understand the etymology of the words I was using. It was time to find out more.

If you search for neurodiversity in a medical context, you'll quickly see that it isn't a medical term. It came about in 1998 via Australian sociologist Judy Singer, in her thesis 'Odd One In'; her 'personal exploration of a new social movement based on neurological diversity'. In the same year, a journalist by the name of Harvey Blume, who was already in dialogue with Singer, thrust her research, and the concept of neurodiversity, into the public domain in a feature for the American publication *The Atlantic*, and it has stuck. Sadly, in recent years, Singer has been the centre of controversy due to her transphobic views, with the neurodivergent community distancing itself from her work. It's harder to pin down the origins of the terms neurodivergent and neurodivergence, though. Most references state that they arose in the year 2000 in a blog by radically neurodivergent activist Kassiane Asasumasu. She has always said that the coining of these two words was to recognise that non-autistic people can experience the world in a way that is similar to autistic people; that they were meant for a broad variety of people, not just those with neurodevelopmental disorders, as is now often the case.

Researchers hypothesise that between 15 and 20 per cent of the global population exhibit some form of neurodivergence. Then you'll see references to the other 80 per cent under another relatively new umbrella term of 'neurotypical'. Again, this is all a question of semantics. Of course, using the word 'typical' is less controversial than using 'normal', but surely every human brain is different anyway, therefore rendering it impossible to label anyone as typical? Interestingly, this term doesn't seem to be attributable to anyone specific, and apparently, its original use was in satire. The mainstream use of the word neurotypical came through the neurodiversity movement itself; perhaps to pigeonhole anyone that didn't display atypical symptoms. For me, each unique observer is going to have a different perception of where the line between divergent and typical falls and ultimately, as we are all neurodiverse, we can diverge in our own way, and that's what makes us unique, right? Ironically, the same arguments of subjectivity and semantics are bleeding into this paragraph. Who am I to judge who is and who isn't neurodivergent? In fact, you could argue, why should anyone?

What sort of diagnoses mean that you're neurodivergent? You can find loads of infographics and lists online that give you a rough idea, but the same conditions repeatedly appear; autism, ADHD and the 'dys's': dyslexia, dyspraxia, dyscalculia and dysgraphia. With this correlation in mind, these will be the five areas of focus for this book. This isn't me wielding some kind of hammer of judgement on what constitutes being neurodivergent, and I don't intend to demean, undermine or downplay the experiences of anyone else. However, if you consider the fact that the whole concept of neurodivergence can be infinite if we define it that way, then I had to set parameters, or I'd never have finished writing this book.

Let's have a look at the conditions I'll be covering, starting with my own: ADHD (attention deficit hyperactivity disorder). The name itself is misleading. It's not a deficit of attention – we often have too much. ADHD is split into three main types: inattentive, hyperactive/impulsive and combined. If you display traits from only one of the first two categories, that's how your ADHD will be diagnosed. If you show six or more traits from both, you'll be diagnosed with the combined type.

The inattentive type is the most common but can be harder to spot because it doesn't fit the stereotype. It's the hyperactive/impulsive type that people tend to envisage when they think of ADHD, mostly thanks to outdated ideas about the condition that focus on the most obvious traits. Someone who is restless, fidgety, constantly talking, impatient, interrupting, and seems to act before thinking. While people with this type might struggle with impulse control and risk-taking, they might not have the same attention issues as those with the inattentive type, who can seem like the opposite. Often coming across as quiet, distracted or daydreamy, the reality is that their brains are often in overdrive. They may struggle to focus, forget things constantly, and flit between tasks. They can make careless mistakes – not because they don't care, but because their attention is scattered. The constant mental effort of keeping up can lead to exhaustion, overwhelm and burnout. Some may also have auditory processing issues, meaning they take longer to process what they hear, which can make listening and following conversations difficult. Did I say they keep forgetting everything?

ADHD symptoms are usually present in childhood, but they're often overlooked or misattributed, especially in girls. In adulthood, some symptoms can intensify, leading to issues like binge eating, risky driving, impulsive spending, or even addiction. Social interactions, relationships and mental health can all be affected. But ADHD isn't unmanageable. It's treatable, and with the right support – whether that's therapy, coping strategies or medication – people can learn to work with their brains rather than against them. Medications, usually stimulant-based, help boost certain brain chemicals, improving focus and reducing some symptoms. They don't suit or work for everyone, but for some, they make a huge difference. ADHD is still under-diagnosed in girls and women. Not only can it present differently but outdated societal perceptions of the condition have traditionally, but wrongly, framed ADHD as something that mainly affects males. That's simply not true, and it's left countless women and girls struggling for recognition, support and diagnosis.

What about autism? The best place to start is the website of the National Autistic Society (NAS). They head up their website landing page with an excellent paragraph defining what autism is: 'A lifelong developmental disability which affects how people communicate and interact with the world.' There's also a similar statement on the NHS website, outlining that autism isn't an illness, there's no specific treatment for it, and there certainly isn't a cure. The NAS also inform us that autism is a 'spectrum' condition, affecting people in different ways. You might be familiar with the term 'spectrum' as autism is also known as 'autism spectrum disorder', or ASD. The use of the word 'disorder' is something we're steering away from, however, as it has negative connotations and is an example of what we call 'disablist' language. Some of the key traits and challenges for autistic people may or may not include difficulties with social communication and/or interaction, highly restrictive and repetitive behaviours (including hobbies and interests), and sensory sensitivity. These can lead to something known as meltdown, which is an intense response to an overwhelming situation. The NAS website states that the public often struggle to differentiate between a meltdown and a 'temper tantrum'. A meltdown is a temporary loss of behavioural control, which can manifest either verbally, physically, or in both ways. This may look like someone screaming, crying or shouting, in conjunction with lashing out physically. Autistic people can also experience the opposite of this as a response to an overwhelming situation, shutting themselves off, refusing to engage and avoiding certain things completely. This is known as 'shutdown'. You may also hear the term 'stimming' in reference to autism. This is short for 'self-stimulation' and refers to repetitive behaviours that people with autism may use to cope in some situations. Some examples of 'stims' can be flapping hands, head-banging and rocking, but there are many others. There are several reasons why autistic people stim. They may do it because they enjoy it, they may be seeking a form of sensory input, or they may be trying to reduce sensory input. Symptoms and behaviours of autism, and of all neurodivergent conditions, can be much harder to notice in girls, as it's thought they develop strategies to hide their differences. This is known as 'masking'. These are all generalisations, though, and it's important to recognise that autism presents differently for each autistic person.

The dys's are four individual diagnoses, but are often put into a group known as 'specific learning disorders', or

SpLDs, for short. It's likely that you've heard of dyslexia, and possibly dyspraxia, but dyscalculia and dysgraphia are less well known.

Dyslexia is a common learning difficulty and generally impacts reading, writing and spelling. That said, it's really a processing disorder, meaning that dyslexic people have difficulties taking in information they hear and see. This then has a knock-on effect on the acquisition of literacy skills. Estimates suggest that 1 in 10 people have a 'degree' of dyslexia. Other symptoms can include difficulties with organisation, sequencing, letter confusion (often b and d) and slow reading and writing speeds. There are many screening tools available for dyslexia that anyone can access, but only people with a level seven qualification in the assessment of specific learning difficulties can carry out a diagnosis. These are usually educational psychologists or people known as 'specialist teachers'. A diagnosis can help someone with specific learning difficulties obtain appropriate support, such as reasonable adjustments to access education and specific adjustments in assessments and examinations, known as exam access arrangements.

You're likely to have heard of dyspraxia, which is also known as developmental coordination disorder (DCD). This affects physical coordination, balance and what we call 'fine' and 'gross' motor skills. It literally means 'difficulty in carrying out an action' and its symptoms are present in childhood but can affect anyone. Medically, dyspraxia represents difficulty with planning and executing movement, and educationally, can include difficulty with spatial perception.

Dyscalculia is defined as a difficulty in understanding numbers and makes mathematics an absolute nightmare. The difficulties symbolic of dyscalculia are complex and may include lack of recognition of the concept of numbers and how they interact with each other, and an inability to use basic functions. Studies in dyscalculia are sparse, and diagnosis is much less common than it is for dyslexia, for example.

Finally, there's dysgraphia, which signifies difficulties with the coordination, coherence and construction of handwriting. However, there are people who don't believe dysgraphia exists, or that it falls under other conditions. Therefore it's a rare diagnosis, and not something that professionals are always willing to consider or explore.

Research suggests that neurodivergent conditions, particularly those I'm focusing on, can often co-occur. Simply put, if you are diagnosed with one condition, it's much more likely you'll have another, and this is the 'comorbidity' mentioned earlier. For example, in recent years, it has become apparent that many people who have an autism diagnosis would also meet the criteria for ADHD. There's a growing body of research evidence to support this correlation. I've found that most of the people I speak to in a professional context who are seeking a diagnosis of one of these, tend to be exploring the other at the same time. This has led to the creation of the portmanteau 'AuDHD' for when the two co-occur, with some people believing that one day it'll become a standalone diagnosis in itself. As it stands, I must be clear that AuDHD isn't a specific diagnostic term. Even so, its use is spreading from within the neurodivergent community to more prominent platforms, and you may come across it. Research also points to a significant overlap between ADHD and the dys's. It's essential we recognise the intersection of neurodivergent conditions whilst acknowledging that the narratives and research around them are still in their infancy.

NO, YOU'RE MACERATING THE MOTH ABDOMENS! 19

So that's the rationale behind the neurodivergence element. Back to moth penises. Well, not literally, but let's take a moment to focus on this book's nature arc. On a personal level, I'm a naturalist with an interest in birds, moths and wildflowers. However, I work in education, not in an environmental or conservation role, so broadening my understanding, experience and exposure was vital. I began widening the search for interviewees who had niche nature obsessions, which soon resulted in a pool of 20, all with a variety of neurodivergent diagnoses and working roles, but not necessarily in outdoor industries. I planned to speak to some online and meet anyone local in person. For a short time, I felt that as many discussions as possible should happen face-to-face. I even negotiated some time away from school to travel to Dorset for three interviews. At this point, I still thought I could write a shortish chapter for each person I met or spoke to. How wrong I was.

This interview process revolved around a set of 21 questions, focusing on a range of themes I thought would become the core of the book. However, when I wrote up the first interview, I found myself struggling to keep it under 5,000 words. I was trying to organise something that could never truly be logical. Unfortunately, it took a long time (nearly a year) to stop, take stock, and accept that what I had set out to do must radically change. Up until that moment, with masses of edginess and some sleepless nights, I was writing two separate book narratives alongside each other with very different formats. It just wasn't tenable. The narrative of this book has often felt like sand in the wind, granular details shifting in fluid movements, which dissipate just when I think they're about to coalesce. I put this down to two factors. One is the organic nature of writing about, well, nature. I would read something or speak to someone, and then the conceptual framework of the book would expand, leading me to obsess about each of these new strands and get lost down rabbit holes for hours on end. My friends, that is how writing about moth penises can metamorphosise into 70,000 words.

I dread to think how much writing time has been lost to reading about things that never made it near the final book. That's the second factor affecting the book: the reality of being neurodivergent myself. What bright spark thought that being neurodivergent and speaking to other neurodivergent people about being neurodivergent themselves would be a good idea? Honestly, amalgamating a million ideas into something that eventually resembles a book is already bloody hard, without having wonky wiring to contend with. To make matters worse, trying to arrange and stick to meeting times when you have ADHD is an absolute nightmare. The coordination of my work and personal calendars, with my interviewee's own ones, and then all the other factors that come into play (work, family etc.) is challenging enough without the added problem of forgetting the calendar exists in the first place. I guess I didn't pre-empt what might happen when two sets of disorganisation met. This also explains the conversational and tangential style in which I write. But it's who I am and it's how my mind connects things. I've done my best to join all the dots into a flowing narrative in a logical way; it just might not be as logical to you as it is to me.

I'm not necessarily blaming my ADHD for all of this, but two of its symptoms happen to be continually starting new tasks before finishing old ones and having poor organisational skills. The former explains my haphazard writing processes, but the latter is an interesting one, as I found myself overcompensating and then trying too hard to organise this book in a linear way. I began to obsess over getting the gender balance right, but then the spread of diagnoses in the book began to skew. It was getting messy, and at times, was freaking me out. Thankfully, the book was organically changing, and out of nowhere came a realisation that I was speaking to at least one neurodivergent employee from each of the major UK conservation charities. Was this a new arc? Could I expand it? No, Joe, don't start thinking about it. Too late. Ooh, this person is sharing a negative experience; I wonder if I can find someone to support or counter their perspective. This rabbit hole quickly became a warren, and I found myself trying to infiltrate these organisations, tapping into professional networks and building a picture, not only of inclusion for neurodivergent people within these organisations, but inclusion for all.

From that point on, the direction of the book was set. More people began coming forward, which led to representation from more organisations. I soon had a more refined set of questions to ask people and was gathering anecdotes about recruitment experiences and reasonable adjustments, as well as general opinions on inclusion. However, this swiftly became my main focus, and I wasn't aware of how far I was drifting from the original person-centred structure. Then I found myself flipping the angle yet again, and began easing this 'organisational probing' and returning to sourcing interviewees. To do this, I had to draw loads of strands together to locate the right people. The easiest way to do this was to use a collective description for those working in outdoor, nature-facing jobs. So, when I put out a request on social media for neurodivergent people who work ... with animals? outdoors? in nature?, no matter the wording choice, it wouldn't stick. What could I call it? The outdoor sector? The ecological? In the end, I went for 'environmental sector'. The experiences and stories of neurodivergent people who work in the environmental sector.

I feel a debt of gratitude towards the people who originally put their heads above the proverbial parapet to contribute their insights and experiences to this book. When I stood at the writing junction, and finally set foot in the direction of travel that follows this opening chapter, I had already held interviews with nine people. I want to take a moment to introduce and thank these nine trailblazers, for laying the foundations for the many others who came after them. I really appreciate that none of them were precious when I explained that I was changing the book structure. The inaugural interviewee was Hazel Jackson, who I met online after connecting through social media. Hazel is the head of conservation outcomes and evidence at the Woodland Trust and has ADHD combined type. The next evening was spent in the online company of Colin Everett, a self-employed ornithological consultant, who is autistic. Then there was another online interview, which was with Emily Clarke. Emily is dyslexic and works as a principal flood and coastal consultant for Binnies, an environmental engineering organisation.

Somewhere in amongst all of this, I drove down to Dorset and met with James Hankins, an agricultural teacher with ADHD. Later the same day, I met with Lucy Morris (and her mum), who edits her own nature magazine, *Conker Nature*, and has dyspraxia. The following day, I spent some time with Lottie Trewick, who works for a nature recovery organisation, and is

NO, YOU'RE MACERATING THE MOTH ABDOMENS! 23

dyslexic. I then spent an evening online with someone else neurodivergent, who features in the book but has chosen to remain anonymous. In these embryonic days, there was also one contributor whose preference was to communicate through email. This vibrant variety of people were all fundamental in shaping this book, and I'm forever grateful to them for this. Yes, it felt traitorous to be changing the book so significantly after doing so much work on it, but it was becoming obvious that there were far more people who should be part of it. You will notice that some of these people, for a range of reasons, have asked not to be named or for me to just use their first name. Speaking out on some of the themes in this book obviously caused some internal conflict in people, and the last thing I wanted was to create anxiety. I have respected their requests for anonymity.

So, that was how it all came about. Starting with the maceration of three moth abdomens and an unintentionally hilarious text message which got me thinking about niche nature obsessions. Traversing onwards along the most overgrown paths imaginable, my thought processes, before winding down into a meadow of coherence where I could focus on what I really wanted this book to become. I've lost count of how many times I've said I'm giving up on this book. It has felt impossible, it has felt unachievable, I've even felt like I'm disassociating from it. That's the point, though. Neurodivergence isn't linear or logical, it flows and meanders, ebbs and pulses, and eventually settles into something akin to regularity. Throughout the rest of this book, please do take time to reflect on the beauty of difference. Join me in celebrating the gorgeously disparate ways that our brains function, and the unique angles and insights we can bring to making connections with the natural world. This book is about people, and where does this journey start for these people who have come forward, identifying as neurodivergent? It starts with some symptoms and then a realisation. Eventually it leads to a label, some clarity, and often some support. We all begin our journey at a similar point, with the same outcome in the distance ahead of us: a formal diagnosis.

CHAPTER TWO

Dia and Gignoskein

Seeking diagnosis

Diagnosis: From the Greek words dia and gignoskein. Meaning 'to recognise apart from another'.

Why does anyone seek a diagnosis in the first place? There's a hint towards one of the reasons in this Greek etymology. To recognise. As a race, we strive to understand ourselves and the world we live in. To make sense of it, we create constructs such as time, money and society. When things deviate from these constructs, we struggle, and when we struggle, we seek answers. A diagnosis is an answer to a problem. A problem that will be having such an impact on our quality of life that we take action to try and improve it; we try to treat and manage it as our constructs inform us we should. As well as treating symptoms, a diagnosis can also validate them. Chronic pain is an example of this: while it is only felt by the sufferer, a diagnosis can breathe identity and reasoning into unmanageable symptoms that no one else can relate to. It's that word, understanding, again. Clarity. Cohesion. Community. Despite the Greek definition of a state of being apart, there's a certain beauty in a diagnosis. Despite enforcing our apartness, it can also bring us closer together.

As well as clarity, there are many other reasons why someone may seek a diagnosis. At school age, a formal diagnosis can oblige education settings to put reasonable adjustments in place. As soon as someone has that piece of paper stating they are 'X' or 'Y', they can choose to identify themselves as having a disability, or those making decisions on their behalf can advocate for them, citing a disability. This shrouds them in a cloak of legality, as disability is one of the nine 'protected characteristics' of the UK Equality Act. It can also support changes in placements and provisions to more appropriate ones, as well as potentially opening access to additional support. Putting these things in place earlier can lead to the easier implementation of adjustments throughout life, like the transition into further- and higher-education settings, and on to the world of work. Ultimately, one of the most important effects of a formal diagnosis is that it should, in theory, ensure the collaborative working of everyone around an individual, whatever their age. For example, an education, health and care plan (EHCP) – a legally binding document – can be put in place for people up to the age of 25, and brings professionals working across these three spheres together to work towards agreed outcomes.

There are many strands that make up the diagnostic process of a neurodevelopmental condition. They're bound by rigorous medical frameworks, with roots in psychiatry, and a deep focus on the presentation of an individual in a variety of settings, scenarios and contexts. They really are all-encompassing. With an adult diagnosis, you must delve into your childhood experiences and construct a life narrative. It might be difficult to open old wounds and reflect on the elements that shape you. You must be ready for this. Ultimately though, the decision to diagnose sits with the consultant in front of you, but who is to say that the next consultant and the next one would hold the same opinion? It's all very subjective. I've met several children in my career who I perceive to present with a specific need, but other professionals disagree. Or I've had to observe someone and don't concur with other professional perceptions.

Again, it's all a case of subjection. It's subjective if you go through the NHS, and it's subjective if you go through a private consultancy.

I do understand the need for alternative pathways. Anecdotally, the wait for both child and adult neurodevelopmental assessments in my home county of Norfolk is a minimum of three years. I often advise parents to consider the private pathway, especially if their child is struggling in school and they're crying out for support from other professionals. Sometimes a diagnosis, from someone who is legally able to supply one, is the biggest leap towards getting any help at all. Requiring additional support is often a driver for seeking a diagnosis in both adults and children, as is the desire for clarity and answers. Again, this is all subjective, as every person has a different, individual reason for seeking a diagnosis. If you're reading this and have been through this process yourself, what was your reason? For many, a catalyst of some sort prompts them to act. It could be an incident, a person, a lightbulb moment, one of many things or multiples of them. For myself, the trigger for the diagnostic process was a single discussion with a person, leading to a cascade of thoughts, actions, reflections and responses. A discussion: succinct, but so powerful in the grand scheme of things.

Several years back, I was working alongside a mental health nurse whose specialism was ADHD. She strode up to me one day, requesting a 'private chat', which wasn't her style at all. She wasn't averse to holding a conversation in earshot of colleagues, so I rationalised that this could be something serious. I was edgy. Closed doors meant something serious. She came into my office, shut the door behind herself, leant over, held eye contact with me and said, 'Have you ever considered that you have ADHD,

Joe?' Those nine words, spoken in a broad West Midlands accent, set my thoughts swirling: simultaneously crashing down and pogoing against the ceiling. How, in all my years of working with neurodivergent young people, had I not made the connection that my wiring was so like theirs? How had nobody else?

I took the first steps towards a diagnosis, but the process was incredibly slow. From asking the doctor to make a referral, to receiving and submitting Conners scales (the initial scoring questionnaire) to the first 90-minute consultation, the wait was three-and-a-half years. The thing is, I knew it, my wife knew it, my workplace was already adjusting for it, and my family didn't challenge it.

What did happen is that I began going through a weird midlife closure process. Negative choices suddenly made sense. Dropping out of sixth form and then college in consecutive years. Getting beaten up several times. Addiction. Debt. Car accidents. The inability to regulate my emotions. The way my brain quickly overloads with information. ADHD was not going to become an excuse, and I actively avoid using it as one, but understanding that my brain is a bit messy offers me a great deal of reassurance. The whole idea *completes* me; that's the only way I can describe it. When that first consultation finally came round, it was 90 minutes, and so was the second. Number one is a 'let's dissect your past' session, and number two is 'let's talk about everything you do that irritates people close to you'. The consultant also spoke to my wife on the phone for 30 minutes. Half an hour to offload how I never complete a task, never listen and can't focus on anything other than what's in front of me. She was loving her time in the ADHD confessional box. After three-and-a-half years of waiting, the diagnosis was made in less than six weeks.

Diagnosis: Attention Deficit Hyperactivity Disorder (ADHD), combined type. November 2022. That's what the letter said, but the confirmation came over the phone weeks before the paperwork landed on the doormat. It only felt surreal for a fleeting moment, then I had a shot of clarity, which ebbed away when the consultant said, 'You're not surprised, are you?' Not in the slightest, I told her, although I was fighting a complex mix of feelings. A bit of shame, a sprinkling of shock, an uneasy feeling of easement, all battling to be at the forefront of my overactive mind. Then a reality check, and one that I suspect many people aren't aware of. I would have to notify the Driver and Vehicle Licensing Agency (DVLA) that I now had a diagnosis of ADHD. Why? If they consider any condition to have an adverse effect on your driving ability, they reserve the right to revoke your licence, or make you retake a driving test. They don't tell you that in the small print! OK, that's a bit innacurate, as they do include it in the diagnostic report as a next step, but unless you'd done your research, you wouldn't know.

I'll be candid with you; there wasn't any radical change or epiphanic moment after this. I'd been living the last three years as though I had ADHD, anyway, putting my own adjustments in place at home and work so I could function. Spend 10 minutes in my company and it's obvious, so it was hardly a surprise to those that know me. It amazes me that it wasn't on my teachers' radars when I was at school; after all, I was the antithesis of a model student. I left secondary school in the early 2000s, which is around the time that research suggests there was an increase in ADHD diagnosis. Unfortunately, it seems that the boom didn't reach Norfolk in time, much like everything else in life, reaching our county a few years later. It isn't worth dwelling on, but perhaps with support in place, the decade after school may have been less of a mess for me. I just flew under the radar, like so many other children in my generation. Instead, in the eyes of society, and my teachers, I was the archetypal product of a single mother in social housing, and of course I was going to act up to that.

I also met my developmental milestones, such as first words, or walking, in a timely fashion during childhood, therefore it was, of course, socio-economics causing my poor behaviour (it's tough to convey sarcasm here). Milestones are a construct of our own design, made to govern what is 'normal' development and what isn't. This measuring begins from birth. There's a market for milestone 'cards', so parents can capture everything on their social-media feeds forever. Science and society place these constraints on our progress, often causing great anxiety to parents of children who develop at a slower rate than their peers. This often becomes more evident as children start interacting with other children, usually in early-years settings, or the first years of school. This is when many parents I've spoken to say they began to see differences in their children. It's worth remembering that we also have a generation of children for whom COVID-19 may impact their social interaction skills in the future. Having concerns, and then acting on them, is only the tip of the metaphorical diagnostic iceberg, though. Once advice has been sought, and referrals made, the waiting begins.

The length of NHS waiting lists remains the biggest barrier to getting a diagnosis of not only ADHD, but also of autism, in the UK. A 2024 healthcare sector study found that just over 130,000 people were awaiting an autism referral at that time, and half of those had been waiting for over a year. The same study supposes that up to 2.6 million people in the UK may have ADHD, with up to 2 million of those not having a diagnosis. Whilst these figures are likely to fluctuate around the data available at the time and not be entirely accurate, what they represent is the length of diagnostic wait times here; something which the report clearly defines as a *crisis*. From my own experience and those of the young people I've taught over the years, this calamitous situation has been brewing for a while. I waited three years. Five years ago, it was at least a year's wait. Even back in 2019, the British Medical Association were critical of autism assessment waiting times, voicing their concerns in a report with the ominous title of 'Failing a Generation'. As you can likely guess, staffing levels, communication and inappropriate referrals were reportedly the drivers – no one takes any responsibility! This lack of communication and collaboration is often a recurring theme in the lives of neurodivergent people, and in this book.

An autism diagnosis is a process that, throughout my career, I've been able to observe and play a direct role in. An autism assessment generally has two components. A developmental commentary, and an observation of this behaviour. The commonest diagnostic tool I've come across is the Autism Diagnostic Observation Schedule (ADOS), which is a *semi-structured, standardised assessment* that looks at current behaviours and skills, and, as the name suggests, is observational. The process usually features some form of interview, the gathering of reports from any other settings or professionals working with the individual under assessment, and the formation of a chronological and familial narrative. As part of my working roles, I've undertaken the completion of school observation paperwork to feed into these assessments. Sometimes it's difficult to connect the dots as an educator, as many autistic young people mask their symptoms in school and conform to expectations and norms. All these inputs coalesce to inform the decision as to whether a diagnosis is appropriate. The NAS website is an incredible source of information regarding the autism diagnostic process, and contains a wealth of information and resources, from a range of perspectives, including education. I thoroughly recommend looking.

What is it like to wait and wait for answers, clarity and support, when you know deep down that you're neurodivergent? This is the limbo-like situation that Barbara finds herself in. A community officer for Berkshire, Buckinghamshire and Oxfordshire Wildlife Trust, she has been on the NHS waiting list for an ADHD assessment for two years, and lives in an area where, like most of the UK, the average NHS wait time for an adult is up to four years. Like many people, Barbara doesn't have access to the £1,000 that it costs to go private. Since childhood, she has always felt different, as though she doesn't fit in with societal norms. She describes herself as a daydreaming, highly empathic and anxious child, with difficulties interacting with people outside her family circle. As neurodiversity wasn't even a concept back then, she just thought she was 'weird and hopeless', and therefore her life has always had an undercurrent of mental health and self-esteem issues, often serious enough to require medical intervention. Then, more recently, her own child went onto the autism diagnostic pathway, which took four years. During this time, Barbara began researching adult neurodiversity and the proverbial penny began to drop.

Similarly to me, Barbara spent several years working in the special educational needs and disabilities (SEND) department of a secondary school but didn't pick up on any signs in herself. She says that once the realisation hit, a lot of things began to make sense, albeit at the tender age of 48. Now she just waits for that confirmation, but as everyone is different, so are their responses to this situation. To some extent she is content that she now has a name for her struggles, understands why traditional medication didn't work for her depression and anxiety, and is finally able to validate her feelings and emotions, instead of simply wearing labels like 'weird', 'hysterical', 'psycho', 'moody', 'crazy', 'exaggerated' or 'grumpy'. This validation isn't only important for Barbara on a personal level, but also on a professional one. Her research has given her a deeper understanding of what makes a conducive environment for neurodivergent people to work in, and a recognition that she has the right to work somewhere that is respectful of her needs. Something, she adds, that she's lucky to experience in her current role, as her employers have been fantastic in supporting her neurodivergence, offering her as much support as they can.

What if the wait for a diagnosis is through choice or circumstance? Take Colin Everett, for example, a consultant ornithologist, who tells me that he only got his autism diagnosis two years ago, at the age of 50. This intrigues me and I ask him what the rationale was, at that age, to seek a diagnosis. He says that he felt it was time to get to know himself better. Colin was given various mislabels in his youth that didn't negatively impact him in the long-term, but were detrimental to his experiences in the education system. Did he always know he was autistic? Yes, he thinks so, but when he was growing up in the 1970s and 1980s, there wasn't really the language to describe what later became known as high-functioning forms of autism. Instead, we had other terms like 'maladjusted'. I squirm at this derogatory term. You wouldn't want an autism diagnosis in the 1970s, he says. Even 50 years ago, autism meant that you were 'mentally retarded' with 'refrigerator mothers' receiving the blame for psychologically damaging their children through lack of affection. Why would anyone want this shame and stigma?

Parental stigma was also a part of Hazel Jackson's diagnosis. Her diagnosis of ADHD combined type (like me) came at the age of 42, 18 months prior to us speaking. It was the second time she'd gone through the process, as several years earlier she'd had an assessment, but didn't follow it through. Why? Mainly because she found herself worrying about how it was making her mum feel. As part of the diagnostic process, her mum would talk to the consultant about Hazel's childhood, and to her it felt like there may be judgements on her parenting. Plus, to her mum, it all meant there was something 'wrong' with Hazel, which obviously brought up some difficult emotions. My mum was the same when I went through my own diagnosis, and Hazel and I discuss how parents perhaps go through a process of denial in these situations. When Hazel did finally get her diagnosis, her mum found out more about ADHD, and as Hazel herself doesn't see it as a negative, her mum has now come round to a similar way of thinking. All Hazel was searching for were solutions to the issues plaguing her through life. She feels that she has now got these solutions.

The 'dys's' are an example of neurodivergence becoming apparent during traditional education, when symptoms often become more overt as we begin learning to read and write and exploring a wider range of motor skills. Take the experiences of Emily Clarke, for example. Her best friend had a dyslexia diagnosis at the age of five and

Emily says that there were many similarities in the barriers they both faced. However, Emily's family were told that she was 'clever' and 'asked too many questions', implying that the issue was her focus and concentration, rather than anything else. Yet at high school, teachers made Emily drop a subject in order to take extra English lessons, with no explanation other than that she was 'struggling'. There was no suggestion that there might be an underlying problem, the implication being that such an issue should have been given recognition long before secondary school. She reflects that her English teacher would come in and lecture, which she just couldn't process, and years later, when her grade prediction was the old 'D' grade and lower than other subjects; her parents chose to query it at a parents' evening. Seventy per cent of Emily's teachers had general concerns despite her higher grades, but no action had been taken.

It's that classic lack of communication and collaboration again, and what I find particularly interesting is that Emily was attending a private school, which had smaller class sizes and therefore, a higher staff-to-pupil ratio. In some ways, it's even more shocking that it wasn't evident to those professionals and dealt with earlier. In the end, Emily acknowledges that she was in a fortunate position where her parents were able to pay for a private diagnosis, which came three days before her 16th birthday. Thankfully, this meant that although many years of possible support in her schooling had gone by, in further and then higher education settings, she didn't have to pursue an 'adult' diagnosis. She reflects on her friend again, who had to have a reassessment at university due to having an 'outdated' childhood diagnosis. I struggle with this idea. You don't just grow out of the symptoms of a neurodivergent condition. Yes, they can manifest in different ways (especially in adolescence), but as you get older, you tend to develop a toolkit of coping strategies for all manner of situations. Ultimately though, these fundamental traits don't just suddenly and magically disappear one day, just because you're now an adult.

I was keen to speak to someone who has a diagnosis of a neurodivergent condition but feels unable or reluctant to disclose it. That person is a member of staff from the Royal Society for the Protection of Birds (RSPB), who had got an autism diagnosis shortly before we spoke. I was keen to find out why they'd made the decision to hide this from their employer and sadly, stigma and perceptions were the driving force. They were born in the 1970s and had a working-class 1980s childhood, where they were either constantly being told not to be different or had people asking why they were different. This made no sense though, as to them, it was everyone else who was odd, and not them. Being 'different' back then meant that you were likely to become a target for bullies. You couldn't be weak and couldn't stand out, so that meant retreating into safety mode – masking. Their recent diagnosis doesn't change them or define their identity, but helps to explain why they've always felt out of place. They reflect that as their career progression took them into more senior management roles, two colleagues were incredibly supportive, showing them how to survive and then thrive in the workplace.

So, it's not the anticipation of colleagues' reactions making this person reticent to disclose their diagnosis. It's more that to share it outside a close personal circle would be to admit to being different; the very thing they've been told not to do. I love their adage that they're making sure they truly understand what it all means for them before they attempt to explain it to others. In this sense, they feel as though they are beginning to understand who they really are, which is a recurring theme among the people I've spoken to with diagnoses in adulthood. Reflecting on their workplace again, they find that being in a senior role allows them to introduce adaptations to their own work, with minimal opposition. For example, it's understood that if they're around colleagues for intense periods, they'll have to follow up with some time working alone; or if they undertake any external speaking, they're given time to recharge afterwards. I can't help but think that their seniority affords what many would perceive as preferential treatment, however, they acknowledge this privilege, they are clear they don't take it as a given and are immeasurably grateful for the support of their employers.

Which takes me back to the original question, as to why they're so reluctant to formally disclose their autism to the RSPB. They're nervous. Why? Stigma still definitely exists; they've read and heard so many stories of how other people's perceptions of you can change after disclosure. They want to share it eventually and think it'll happen soon, particularly in the hope that it will show colleagues and new people coming into the organisation and sector that you can be a successful senior leader and be autistic. Although again, they acknowledge the power and importance of having a supportive organisational culture around you; especially to be able to own your adjustments and make them happen. Our conversation ends with two pertinent thoughts from them: We are all unique and therefore so are the solutions, but maybe, if by speaking out, we help to remove some of the myths and the stigma that remain for so many, then maybe more senior managers and leaders will speak out too. They close with some powerful rhetoric: Why should anyone understand all of this, anyway? They're only just starting to, and they're autistic!

Sometimes the catalyst for a diagnosis comes from closer to home. Alister Harman, a National Trust ranger in the north of England, says that he and his parents were aware of his autism from an early age. How? Obviously because of his presentation, also because his siblings have significant special educational needs, therefore his parents were naturally more aware. There are many studies into the occurrence of autism in siblings, and the resounding conclusion is that there is an increased likelihood of a sibling being autistic when another is. Frustratingly, each study seems to produce a different figure for this likelihood, so it's impossible to be definitive. Alister feels that speech and language services were reluctant to pursue a diagnosis for him, as he believes that they didn't want to put in even more support for his family at a higher cost. From the age of five, Alister deliberately kept a low profile, feeling that his siblings' needs were more important than his own. It wasn't until he was 16 that he finally sought an autism diagnosis, when the environment and pressure of school became too much. As he says, when things aren't working, you must change something.

Tracey Churcher, a general manager at the National Trust's Isle of Purbeck property, is another person whose familial situation became the catalyst for her own diagnosis. Tracey grew up with adoptive parents, but as she got older, she began to research her birth mother, and when she found her, she discovered that she had a brother in America, who was 20 years younger than her. She then found out that her brother has ADHD, and as she got to know him, she began recognising his traits in her own children. Subsequently, Tracey began following the diagnostic pathway with her own children, and as she learnt more about ADHD, it became abundantly clear that she also has it. Receiving a diagnosis in her forties, she says that by then, she could 'drive her own bus', as she'd been living and coping with it for so long. However, coming from a background in psychology, she felt like a lot of patterns and ways of thinking suddenly made more sense. She refers to all of this as a journey of discovery, which I think will chime with many neurodivergent people reading this; a journey that seems to be never-ending.

Imagine living your life with all the symptoms and traits of a condition that you don't have a diagnosis for, or even realise that you might have? This is how it is for so many people, and the effect on their quality of life can be vast. Immeasurable, even. The impact is often felt from a young age. The educational experience of neurodivergent young people without diagnosis can often be unnecessarily negative. Unmet needs can lead to labels such as 'disruptive' and 'challenging', which can stick to a child long after they have left the education system. So begins a domino effect on every aspect of someone's life. This initial negative labelling is one of the root forms of educational exclusion. Education, whether it works systemically or not, still provides myriad social and experiential learning opportunities, the exclusion from which can have untold impacts on development. With age, the effects seem to embed into two domains: psychosocial and lifestyle. Mental health issues are common, which can obviously lead to long-term difficulties with forming and maintaining relationships. Addiction, substance abuse and excessive risk-taking can be rife in adulthood; in fact, substance abuse is statistically the most common comorbid psychiatric disorder in adults with ADHD.

The diagnosis of neurodivergent conditions is a huge topic, and one which I can only scratch the surface of here. There are swathes of nuance, meaning that there is variation in individual responses. For many people, it's a positive thing, and most people I've spoken with consider it to be just this. One of the overarching messages from this is that the understanding, clarity and identity brought from finally receiving a diagnosis has been at least life-affirming, and sometimes life-changing. Identity can lead to community, and networks can support, advise and advocate in ways that people may not have been able to access before. Along with validation, a diagnosis may also allow someone to access specific interventions, such as therapies and medication, or request adjustments in the workplace. Of course, these changes may then bring a range of further benefits to the individual across all areas of life, from enhancing overall wellbeing, to improving sleeping patterns, for example. But a diagnosis can also have a darker side. Stigma is still rife across society, and systemic barriers also exist, making the seeking of the diagnosis one act, but the disclosure of it something far more complex.

Awareness and action can be positive for people who have, up until recently, been largely misunderstood. There has been a dramatic rise in people seeking diagnoses of autism and ADHD, seemingly through the increasing representation of neurodivergent people on social media, especially on the platform TikTok. As with anything online, there can be a lot of generalisation and simplification, but overall, it seems to help people feel less alone or separate from society in general. The societal shift in cognizance towards neurodivergence is palpable now. I'm hopeful that the ongoing destigmatisation of neurodivergence continues to allow more people to feel safe and comfortable in who they are. I hope that society continues to become more accepting and accessible for neurodivergent people and accept that a lot of this is down to those people who put their own experiences in the public domain to support others. For so many of us who are neurodivergent, our differences become glaringly apparent at some point, often when we move into more formal education settings, and that's where we're heading next. Back to school.

CHAPTER THREE

Intolerable tyrants in the dock of the kangaroo court

Experiences in education

Through working inside British education, it's impossible for me not to see the conflict between its systems and the needs of neurodivergent young people. If you need something different, you're not going to get it. Schools that are part of larger multi-academy trusts tend to approach teaching and behaviour management in a totalitarian way, with little room for negotiation on expectations.

It's not easy to be different from your peers, and it's even more difficult when standing out makes you even more visible due to your school's stringent culture of quasi-control. It's a culture that's scarily formulaic, cloning itself into a carbon copy of what the so-called 'best' educational establishments look like. Best for whom? Not neurodivergent students, but executives sitting atop pyramidic-like hierarchies, distant from the classroom and receiving salaries that sting your eyes if they ever appear in the media. Machines are great at making more machines, so if you are willing and able to conform, you're more likely to succeed – at least that's what you're taught. In these superficial environments, relationships are supposedly key, yet lack depth. Teaching is rhythmic and formulaic. Expression is non-existent. Is it any wonder so many young people dislike school?

Why do I teach, then? Well, my own experience in education wasn't particularly great. My granny was a year-five teacher at my primary school, so that, and my socioeconomic background, made me a perfect target for bullies. There's a narrative when you have a relative teaching in the same school you attend. One that says you're going to conform and be a model example of that school's culture. Was I going to do that? Of course not; I chose to rebel against it and be difficult and disruptive. This got worse in secondary school, where the children of deprivation stand out more as the emphasis on identity and image deepens with adolescence. I became a self-fulfilling prophecy – the kid from social housing who lives with a single parent and perpetually misbehaves. I can reflect on some of my behaviours now I know I have ADHD, and accept that they weren't all deliberate, but many were. I should have left with nothing, but a handful of teachers didn't give up on me when I'd given up on myself. They saw something that I couldn't see, despite the fact I was defiant, rude and deceitful to them. Those people are why I teach.

If you had a relatively uneventful time at school, as so many people do, I suppose that my experience might seem a bit raucous. However, throughout my career, I've taught children whose stories far outweigh my own. Narratives built on themes of abuse, bereavement, neglect, serious crime and worse. These children are the forgotten. They are the 'excluded', and not just in a figurative sense, but literally too. In 2022, almost half of all children in receipt of a permanent school exclusion in England had a special educational need. I've seen it happen so many times. A child's needs can't be met, things escalate, and it ends with permanent exclusion. These children often end up in the 'school exclusion to prison pipeline', finding themselves in provisions with other vulnerable young people. The risk of exploitation and criminality increases purely through association.

Imagine that you're neurodivergent as well. As poor emotional regulation and challenging behaviour tend to be hallmarks of neurodivergent conditions, the risk of exclusion is much higher. Exclusion, or lack of inclusion, is systemic in the current education system. It has been this way for decades. Underfunding. Lack of training. A recruitment crisis. The whole thing is a bit of a mess, really.

When I sit by the river Stour with Lucy Morris and her mum, Sally, I hear an all-too-familiar story about a failing system. Born prematurely, deaf, and requiring heart surgery, which led to a collapsed lung, it wasn't an easy start for Lucy and her parents. As a toddler, she showed signs of slow development, and several professionals saw her, including speech and language therapists, but in rural Wales, advice was scant and as her needs were being met in the small classes of her local primary school, she never met the infamous 'threshold' for support. In fact, many of Lucy's developmental delays, speech and language problems, and struggles with maths, were put down to her deafness. She got through primary school and went to the local secondary school, but with neither a transition package nor additional support in place, it didn't go well. Bullying began in year seven, and then happened what she describes as one of the most impactfully negative moments in that school. A teacher made her come up to the front of the class and demonstrate a calculation, which she couldn't do. It still troubles her now, which is clear in her wrought expression as she shares it.

Lucy went through somewhat of a metamorphosis in Year 8 after moving to another school, with some older relatives attending too. Her confidence grew with this support around her, and she was made head girl.

Despite growing socially, she was still struggling with learning and receiving nothing in the way of additional intervention. Eventually, her parents made the difficult decision to move to the south of England in the hope of improving their family lifestyle, including better support for Lucy. It was a horrendous time. The bullying there was even more despicable; for example, her hearing aids were physically removed by the perpetrators. A man also came up to her at a bus stop, who later that day went on to violently attack two other people. Lucy had to give evidence to the police, and the whole experience was so traumatic that she shut down, experiencing acute anxiety and suicidal thoughts, all while being in the mid-stages of puberty. It was a dark time for the whole family. Sally always knew there was more to Lucy's needs than her deafness, and at this point of crisis, finally something was put in place, through adolescent mental health services, who began some therapeutic family sessions. This became the first tentative step towards meaningful intervention, after so many difficult years.

At this dark point in the story, some light distraction comes via a song thrush that's belting out a sonata from the trees behind us. This one is verging on nightingale territory, dropping into reels of subsong between each fluting burst. Lucy speaks first, adding that she already knew she was different, but at this time, she was becoming acutely aware of it. Her parents took her out of the original secondary school and the council began trying to place her elsewhere. Thankfully, at this point, the person working with them from mental health services had a chat with Lucy's parents, wondering if an educational psychologist could see Lucy. They said yes. This professional was shocked by Lucy's presentation and that she'd been this way since primary school, with no support. On asking her parents who they should contact to be able to feed into Lucy's EHCP, their blank looks said it all. They didn't even know what such a thing was. That was when a new ball began rolling, towards the most appropriate support for Lucy, but at what cost? It was a positive step, but it took far too long to get there.

Lucy went to an all-girls school for a few months, but the special educational needs department (and the school) weren't at all supportive, so her parents eventually decided to remove her from the school and educate her at home instead. For almost 90,000 children in the UK, homeschooling is the only way they can access either the education they need, or what their parents would prefer. Sally is clear that this decision wasn't taken lightly, as the commitment is huge, and home education isn't always the holistic experience it can be made out to be. This period out of school put up even more barriers: Lucy's preferred post-16 destination was reluctant to offer her a place, due to missing so much school and not sitting any GCSEs. It was at this time that she finally got a diagnosis of dyspraxia, and this was only because she was seen by an occupational therapist who was adamant someone should be looking into it. When a consultant said no, this occupational therapist stood her ground and fought to get Lucy the support that she should have had for the past 10 years.

Lucy's educational journey is not uncommon; I've come across many that are similar throughout my career. The education and health sectors are meant to work in tandem, but both suffer from systemic funding and staffing problems. Of course, the rigid systems in most mainstream schools help to streamline resources and costs, but these one-size-fits-all approaches just marginalise those who face existing barriers even more. Lucy's story is a difficult read. Throughout her education, there have been recurrent failings by multiple professionals and institutions. This failure to identify and support individual needs is an artefact of our social history. If we look back to the 1970s, people with neurodevelopmental conditions were the underbelly of society. This was a time when you might be fed sedatives and put in an institution just to keep you out of sight and mind. Autism, for example, was widely thought to only be a childhood disorder. If you think Lucy's experience was bitter enough, wait for the unrelenting sourness of the next one.

Colin and I established through our early discussions that we wouldn't meet in person. He lives in Wales, and with my own commitments, it felt unrealistic to try and visit him. When he first contacted me, he shared that his diagnosis of autism came at the age of 50. I couldn't stop thinking about this. How do you approach such a potentially significant change to your identity at an age where – I assume – you know who you are? As well as my usual questions, I yearned to find out everything leading up to this point: his presentation as a child, his actual childhood, and his experiences of education at a time when I know that special educational needs were not even a 'thing'. I didn't really know what I was expecting him to say, or if he'd even be forthcoming with such personal information. However, he didn't hide anything, and it ended up being absolute dynamite.

Early on in our conversation, Colin alluded to not having had a particularly enjoyable experience at school, but I chose not to push him. Eventually the theme of education came up and I asked him what his experience at school was like. Hellish, he said. He struggled through primary school with what he described as 'a lot of issues'. For example, he was unable to eat in the dining hall for several reasons: the interactions of the other children; the physical proximity to them; the smell of the food, which was often overpowering, and the taste of it, which was generally disgusting. He would usually just sit there, unable to eat and often in tears. Colin was describing what sounded to me like a sensory processing disorder. He agreed. But back then, adults and peers would simply query what was wrong with 'that boy' and do nothing. This angered us both. Reflecting on this time was painful. It shouldn't have been like that, and we both knew it. Things are better now, much better, but you can't just gloss over the past. Colin's needs were simply not being met.

He got through primary school, but what about secondary? There was some confusion over which school he was going to. Would it be one further away, but with a better reputation, despite neither of his parents having a car to get there? Or would it be another nearby, but notoriously inadequate school? You can guess. After the first term, his attendance fell drastically, and his behaviour became so difficult that the label 'maladjusted' became his designation. He recalls a science lesson where he couldn't cope with the noise and teasing from his peers, so he broke some equipment and got a suspension. He said that everyone kept saying they were 'bending over backwards to deal with him', but from Colin's perspective, he was the one constantly making concessions for an unreasonable and unfriendly world. Within a year, Colin was put in a boarding school for 'maladjusted boys', with 50 boys on roll. Looking back, he surmised that at least 10 of them, although easily more, would now 'have' autism; and many, if not most of the rest, would have ADHD. My mind, personally and professionally, was blown. I wondered what the school was like to attend.

Very complex, he said. It had its own system of self-governance in the form of an internal court, where the boys dealt collectively with each other's grievances. Colin says this was no 'kangaroo court', and staff were always present to guide them. This communal approach bled through the school. Clubs and committees were distinctive and compulsory elements, with the expectation that students took on the roles of chairmen or secretaries. High levels of responsibility were an expectation for all. It seemed progressive to me, but did it work? For some, he mused, but not for him. Many 'old boys' speak highly of the school, but for Colin, it was overwhelming, with social interactions, cues and constructs flying at him from all angles. Did it close under a cloud, like so many institutions from that time? Not at all. Colin went there from 1985 to 1989, and it shut down in 1992. He thinks this was mainly due to the cost of placing boys there. It was said that the fees were as expensive as those at Eton. This wasn't a surprise to me, as the independent specialist education sector still charges astronomical fees to place pupils. It has evidently been this way for a long time.

Early in my research, I came across an article on the Countryside Jobs Service website about discriminatory interview practices, particularly in the conservation sector. This was the moment I came across Alister Harman, and based on his article, I knew immediately that I had to speak to him. Alister was willing to participate in an interview, but logistics and time got in the way of us meeting in person. Then timings and a bereavement further inhibited us from even an online chat. Alister was happy to answer my questions in writing and when I finally received his responses, they were fascinating, moving, blunt, yet eloquent. His experience at secondary school, especially given my own job, is bitterly powerful. He described going to school as wading through a socially and educationally dull quagmire, and details frequent issues conforming to 'this meta-ethereal thing called the curriculum'. Alister never really got to grips with the expectations of school, completing his homework by homing in on anything he knew about the subject in question, rather than the specifics being taught. He says that he was barely scraping through each class, and this is how his GCSEs went. He just didn't fit school, in the traditional sense.

It also didn't help that Alister saw most of his peers as 'intolerable tyrants'. Going into school each day, the prospect of being the victim of some kind of attack, or bullying, became his normal. He felt so hyper-aware to danger at school that he could often tell if someone was going to jump him just by the atmosphere in the area. Interestingly, he says that he still gets this sense in some situations, describing it as strangely comforting, if exhausting. He doesn't shy away from the fact that he was a target for an awful lot of bullying. However, he also (somewhat unfortunately) had the accolade of being one of the stronger fighters in the school. Alister had a rule; if someone hit him, then he would be the one ending the fight. He's clear that he really did end them, as being on the receiving end of that level of abuse does one of two things to you, either you break, or you fight back. Alister described the day he finally left school for good as one of the best days of his life.

What if you manage through school and further education, but your symptoms and problems come to the fore in higher education? This was the experience of Lottie Trewick, who I met at the base of St Catherine's Hill in Winchester. She couldn't meet me until late morning, so I was able to spend a few hours on the ancient slopes, searching for orchids and butterflies. This chalk downland site is overseen by Hampshire Wildlife Trust, and on a sunny day is teeming with life. I was hoping to encounter at least one species of orchid and butterfly there that I hadn't seen before and the initial omens of the natural world bade well. Stepping onto a narrow path by the reserve entrance, I heard the rapid and shrill song of a firecrest emanating from some thick scrub. There it sat, singing from an eye-level perch with its flaming orange crest flicking up. Tight purple clusters of pyramidal orchids were lining the trackside by my feet. It felt so blissful and exciting there, filling me with an overwhelming sense of warmth and comfort. My target butterfly species, the marbled white, was beckoning me on. It didn't take long to get my first proper look at one.

I headed along the western side of the hill, where the sloping banks are a haven for wildflowers. Lurid yellow rough hawksbit vied for space among the masses of oxeye daisies. Taking a deeper look, I could see the explosive supernovas of flowering clover closer to the ground. Butterflies flitted by and there were at least two grizzled skippers on this ridge; a species only found at two sites in my native Norfolk. The marbled white doesn't occur at any site at all. At the south-west corner of the hill sat a dense clump of wildflowers, somewhere between knee and waist height, with a path hewn through the middle. Butterflies were everywhere in this sunny enclave, and many of them were marbled whites. I couldn't take my eyes off them, they were glorious. Their mock-Tudor upper wings are vibrant, yes, but the dull marbling on the underwing is the clincher for me, and just as exquisite. As is always the case with a new species, I spent some time observing and absorbing their nuances. They're beautiful, but not in a gaudy way. In all the excitement, I'd lost track of time.

I really had to return to where I began, so I decided to walk up and over the hill and take in the view. This meant traversing the southern slope, which, according to my research was the best place to spot the rarer species of orchid that grow on the reserve. Any of these would be a new one for me: frog, musk, and autumn lady's-tresses; but I drew a blank. Even halfway up, the view was astonishing. The hospital of St. Cross sits in the water meadows to the west, and looking to the base of the southern slopes, I could see the scarring of a more macabre history. This is 'plague pits valley', and its name leaves little to the imagination. The linear markings were mass graves. At the apex, the meadows rolled away, the river wobbled in the heat haze and I was taken aback by the beauty of it all. These higher climes hide the ramparts of an Iron-Age hill fort and I was struck by the appeal of a single place; for people with a variety of interests it's truly a remarkable place to visit. The time! I bounded down the north-west descent, on ancient chalky paths, conscious of being late.

I made it to the Handlebar Café, a squat wooden building striding the top of an old bridge, in time for some lunch and an excellent coffee. Lottie arrived. We chatted for a bit, and then she suggested that we walk down to Winchester College water meadows. We strolled for a while and then sat on the lush grass along the clear waters of the river Itchen. It was a wonderful backdrop for an interview. Lottie was 19 and studying physics at university when she got her diagnosis of dyslexia. I was keen to find out just how this came about. She had sat next to a mature student, who at a previous university had found out they were dyslexic and got a diagnosis. She found herself chatting to him and sharing some of her own struggles, her main issue being an inability to keep up with and follow what people are saying, almost like she can't hear them. Obviously useful in a lecture! He told her these were the issues he had been having before, and I added that as a SEND professional, I was recognising what are known as phonological processing issues. 'Yes, I'm phonologically dyslexic,' she said. It made complete sense.

We talked about the many misconceptions around dyslexia, the principal one being how some people think it means that someone can't read or write. As she said, Lottie's biggest problem was when she was part of a conversation with multiple people. She described how confusing it could be for her: 'Someone over there talking, someone over there talking, there's a bird over there, I can hear that as well, and I'm trying so hard to listen to the person that's talking to me, but my brain is like ping, ping, ping, picking up everything else.' She worries that people think she's being rude when there are a thousand thoughts going through her head distracting her. This is a common affliction for neurodivergent people. We're not rude, our brains are just fizzing all over the place. How did she get support in the end? After speaking to her dyslexic peer, she went to the internal adjustment unit at university, who, after speaking to her, were confident that she may, indeed, be dyslexic, and paid for a diagnostic assessment. A diagnosis didn't change much for Lottie, other than allowing her additional time in exams, but like so many others, it gave her clarity and perspective.

Whilst in Dorset, I also met with James Hankins in Blandford Forum, a quaint and busy little town by the river Stour. James was one of the most fascinating people I met whilst writing this book. We had a lot in common, yet had very different experiences of everything, especially education. We clicked immediately, clocking each other as he rolled up – yes rolled up – on a kneel-on scooter, the likes of which I'd never seen before. We ordered some coffees from our meeting point, the trendy Black Cactus café, and utilised the outside seating area as they brewed. He asked me if I had sleeves. Why? To protect myself against the Blandford fly. I honestly thought he was having me on as he explained that Blandford has its own species of biting fly that can cause swelling, redness and fever. Exclusive to the area around the river, its numbers were reduced in the late 1980s when the local authority hit the banks with some hardcore insecticide. However, James assured me that the Blandford fly is returning. I kept laughing at the absurdity of the story, and searched for it online. It's real. I love this guy already.

We walked to the realm of the biting fly and sat on a bench adjacent to a wildflower meadow. Next to us was a high grassy bank, and on the other side was the Badger Brewery, which we both found hilarious as we discussed our histories of alcohol issues. James shared that he works in but also went to a Steiner school. Steiner schools deliver an approach known as Steiner Waldorf education, an alternative method of teaching and learning, with its roots in the ideas of twentieth-century Austrian philosopher, Rudolf Steiner. He saw humans as 'a complex interaction of body, mind and spirit', and these became the three foundations on which he built his educational approach. Holistic and nurturing, the curriculum is described as creative, collaborative and communicative, but what was it like for James? Magical; particularly the way that seasonal transitions were woven in, helping to further embed nature connection. He's also a fan of the block learning format, where a topic is delivered in short intensive chunks to maximise interaction and engagement, for core subjects and the nurturing of creativity. Plus, he learnt languages and music from an early age, went on annual camping trips and regularly performed in large-scale theatre productions. It does sound awesome on paper.

As well as James's comments, if you read into the Steiner approach, many websites refer to an emphasis on nature and the environment. I asked James if this was true for the Steiner school he went to, and he replied 'very much so'. He described how the school was in some outbuildings around a large farmyard and cottage garden, and next door to a farming estate, which had two dairies. A short distance away was the school founders' stately home and estate, containing the school theatre, lots of safe open space and accessible woodland. Being in this wood during the changing of the seasons was very important to James, also serving as the inspiration for numerous activities, games and learning opportunities. He was also able to learn about the workings of the farm and had a lot of interaction with the farmers, missing lessons to watch farm machinery in action during the spring. James has strong memories of many activities, such as the constant search for the elusive four-leaf clover, or stones with holes through them to sell to parents after school and raise money for charity. There's no denying that the organic simplicity of the Steiner school approach sounds wonderful.

I began this chapter by discussing the current educational climate in Britain, and clearly, the Steiner schools are the antithesis of this. Roughly 20 per cent of young people are 'persistently absent from school', which is described as them missing from 10 per cent or more of their possible sessions, roughly equating to 19 days. National school absence data indicates that young people with special educational needs and disabilities are more likely to be persistently absent. Research suggests that a whopping 92 per cent of young people currently experiencing school distress are likely to be neurodivergent, with 83 per cent of those being autistic. It's safe to say that the current education system is not built for neurodivergent people. These 'missing' pupils have been given various medical labels. They've been known as non-attenders and school refusers; then they got their own acronym, EBSA, which stands for emotionally based school avoidance. However, the semantics of the word 'avoidance' wasn't appropriate and the acronym became EBSNA, or emotionally based school non-attendance. Lots of extra labels, for children who probably already have a load of labels, whose parents often end up getting a fine because their child simply can't cope with being at their school.

As I wrote in the opening paragraph of this chapter, the dictatorial systems that currently govern most of our schools just don't seem to work for lots of the children attending them. Interestingly, they do seem to work for most of the neurodivergent children I work with, but the stringent routine and structure works alongside having access to a safe space, emotionally available adults, and an ability to collapse the curriculum as is necessary. Wonderful, of course, but only achievable with additional funding and resources. It isn't just rigid structure that some children find difficult. Since 2018 at least, a narrative exists that our current curricular approach stifles creativity by placing so much emphasis on English, maths and science over, say, drama and art. Learning experiences can be formulaic and emotionless, set to impart the information necessary to pass an exam, rather than to cultivate self-expression. Is it any wonder that children don't want to be a part of it? After all, being a part of something is the very meaning of inclusion, isn't it? Yes, there are fantastic schools and teachers all over the country, but systemically, the expectations on our schools today aren't conducive to teachers' wellbeing, let alone the wellbeing of those they're meant to be teaching.

In the 1970s, if you were presenting as neurodivergent, you might be put out of the way in an institution. When I went to school in the 1990s, you would probably end up in a pupil referral unit, separated from your peers. Now, you are either excluded or stop attending altogether. I know these are generalisations, but I see it all the time. What needs to change? As I reflect on my own experiences and career in education, there are certain things that I know really do work with the hardest-to-reach young people. My 'favourite' teachers took the time to build positive relationships. The best learning I've seen happens when characterful teachers, with years of genuine life experience, are given flexibility over their curricular offers. Sometimes, the pathway must change. GCSEs are not for everyone, and sometimes skills and vocational offers are a better fit. So too are various modular certification frameworks, which can be geared towards specific interests, as the most meaningful learning often is. Most importantly, over and over, I've seen how equitable access to the natural world can be a game-changer for young people, particularly those who are neurodivergent. I find myself wondering why.

CHAPTER FOUR

Hugging a tree for a dopamine fix

The importance of nature

The benefits of fostering a deep connection with nature, and of spending time outdoors, have been proven repeatedly. A brief view of greenery from an urban window can be rejuvenating. A walk near a body of water, equally so. The return of the blackbird song as spring awakes from its turgid slumber, signalling lighter and longer days, heralds the beginning of improvements in low mood for lots of us. Many revere these moments and experiences, yet many others are unaware of them, despite the well-established notion that connecting with nature has the capacity to offer us all some respite from our frenetic world. Following my own extensive mental health challenges, spending time outside watching birds became a fundamental feature of my own self-care package. To say that I was merely watching birds is a disservice, as birdwatching is an immersive, multisensory activity that simultaneously stimulates and soothes our brains. I find my solace and comfort through the regularity and seasonal consistency of the natural world. Many people feel the same, and it's difficult to deny the growth in promoting nature connections within therapeutic contexts.

For many years, I've been viewing the benefits of nature connection though the lens of mental health. So much so that it became the theme of my first book, *Bird Therapy*; an exploration of how birdwatching became such a positive factor in my own (ongoing) recovery. Whilst reading into this subject, I fell headlong into yet another rabbit hole; no, a warren, of research papers and articles to try and support my developing perspective. One piece still stands out: 'Natural Thinking' by Dr William Bird. Despite looking at it from a wellbeing angle, I remember it having sections covering ADHD and autism. Working in special education, I recall the empowering feeling of reading this, especially as I had been gently sharing my new interest with some of the young people I was working with at the time. Little did I know that seven years later this would become not only a pleasant connection to my career, but that I would also read it back and reflect on my own neurodivergent diagnosis. It set off a deeper contemplation of the reasons why being in, being with, and connecting to nature feels so important to me and many others who struggle.

With this fresh outlook, much reading, and even more ruminating, I reached the conclusion that my ongoing issues with poor mental health may have been because of underlying ADHD. I'm not saying that my diagnosis suddenly solved all these problems, far from it, but the clarity that the label gives me does, at the very least, help me to make a little more sense of the way my brain and emotions interact and react. My 20-year battle with low mood, acute anxiety and obsessive thoughts takes on a bit of coherence now. Interestingly, a 2017 study found that almost 80 per cent of adults with a diagnosis of ADHD have at least one comorbid psychiatric disorder. So perhaps my innate need to be outside to truly self-regulate is not to manage my mental health symptoms, as I originally thought, but to manage the symptoms of my ADHD that, in turn, have an adverse effect on my mental health. Wherever the symptoms arise from, the benefits of nature connection are numerous and wide-ranging. Water, woodland and wildlife all play their part in the web of wild wellbeing that we are a part of, and that sustains so many of us.

What about ADHD specifically? It's worth pointing out how little research exists into the benefits of being outdoors and connecting with nature, for neurodivergent individuals in a general sense, besides a few literature reviews. The smattering of ADHD-specific research studies available seem to only use small groups of participants. This could be for many reasons, although I do wonder if the stigma around disclosure affects the take-up of these studies. The study with the most citations is an older one from 2004 that explores exposure to nature as a potential 'treatment' for ADHD. This concludes that exposure to natural views and settings may reduce inattention and impulsivity in those without ADHD. However, the control group was small and made up of children, and whilst the findings of this study might similarly apply to adults, the authors are keen to emphasise that there have been minimal studies into exposure to nature for adults with ADHD. It's somewhat disappointing, but understandable, that much of the existing research focuses on young people. What this means is that despite being the most notable study in this area, it's still just a piece of anecdotal conjecture adding meagre weight to the overall evidence base.

In contrast is a piece of research from 2010, where two groups of young people were seen performing better on a concentration task in a woodland setting than in an urban one. Interestingly, they also saw more overall positive behaviour in the woodland setting. Disparity in general wellbeing between urban and rural settings is also found in some research from the following year, where in a series of MRI scans, clear differences were found in the brains of urban-dwelling people. Their amygdalas, the part of the brain that deals with threat, was much more responsive. Overall, they found that people who reside in an urban area for over 15 years can show changes in areas of the brain that regulate stress and threat responses. It's unfortunate that so many of us feel we have to place ourselves in a more stressful and potentially threatening location, albeit that these stresses and threats are of our own making. In these two examples alone, it's evident that hugging trees can give us more than just the brief dopamine hit we're told it does. We may as well just cling on to them for eternity.

I have long thought of the outdoors as an escape. A distraction from everyday life. My safe space. It allows me to unload whatever's clogging my mind, park it wherever I am, focus on something else for however long I feel I need to, and then return to that original headspace with a clearer outlook. I'm refocusing my attention yet resting my brain at the same time. What this is, is a rudimentary description of the attention restoration theory (ART), which came from the work of Stephen and Rachel Kaplan in the late 1980s and early 1990s. They felt that we experience fatigue after any lengthy mental effort, for example, concentrating under academic examination conditions. This became known as 'directed attention', as ultimately that's what we're doing; we're channelling our attention toward a specific action, task or outcome, in a deliberate and voluntary manner. All this effort inevitably makes our brain feel like it needs a rest, and this is where the Kaplans next idea arises. They call this mental lethargy 'directed attention fatigue' (DAF), believing that when we are in this state, we are more prone to human error, which increases our risk of vulnerability.

When you have ADHD, your brain strains as it directs attention to multiple things at once. If we don't manage it, we all react differently, but most people will either melt down or shut down, which is to either outburst externally or close ranks internally. How can we manage this? We can put loads of strategies and adjustments in place, but guess what the Kaplans found can help to restore you when you're experiencing DAF? Of course, being in natural environments. Well, not so much the environment itself, but a series of factors or elements that a natural environment must contain to render it 'restorative'. The first is that it must be 'away', although the Kaplans are clear that being away can range from as little as looking at something different, to being in an actual different environment. Secondly, it must have 'extent', which is how much we are able to immerse ourselves in an environment. The third is that it must have compatibility, with yourself and your motivations for being there, so that you're congruent with it. The final element of a restorative environment is that it mustn't require you to have to deliberately focus on it, something which the Kaplans name 'fascination'.

When I think about being outside myself, I default to thinking about the places I refer to as my 'patches'. Places I've taken pseudo ownership of in my head, that I regularly visit, observe, and collate records for. With each place that takes on this significance comes a deep connection. An understanding of how, when and where certain things will happen, and species can be seen. They've always been somewhere *away*. Somewhere I can escape to and into. They've all had *extent*, in that despite being spread over wide geographic areas, each one was chosen with biodiversity in mind. If your main motivation is to visit a place, get to know it intimately, and then observe its resident wildlife, then you're going to be seeking out a place with that sort of *compatibility* and *extent*. You're naturally going to gravitate toward the natural, the biodiverse. This relationship between myself and a place is important to me. It's vital. However, that importance took on a different meaning after my ADHD diagnosis. I knew I sought these places to restore my wellbeing, but now I know that this happens because these places restore my ADHD brain. It's incredible really.

When I reflect on autism and the outdoors, I can't consider it using personal experiences as I can with ADHD, but I can reflect on it through the prism of professional experience I have from working in the education sector. In all my teaching roles, I have found myself working with young people with special educational needs and disabilities, a large proportion of whom have a diagnosis of autism. Some of these already have an interest in the natural world and many haven't, but none are negative about my hobbies when we've discussed them. In fact, they've embraced them, and we've made wildlife ponds, wildflower seed bombs and bug hotels. We've watched and counted birds, at school and further afield. We've made art from natural items and written about nature and its sensory wonder. In all these outdoor or nature themed activities, I've seen a side of these students that is never shown in a classroom. It's a side of them that's calmer and less vigilant. It's as though they are suddenly more in tune with their surroundings and thus more in tune with themselves.

The predictability of natural environments offers much solace. Flora and fauna move in cycles throughout the year, creating a calendar that one can familiarise themselves and connect with. These routines are logical. They offer a consistency so rarely found in our own species. I suppose that what the natural world becomes is that 'safe space'; a notion seen regularly in the realm of special educational needs. A non-judgemental place where people can be themselves without fear of ridicule. It's accessible at your own pace and on your own terms, things that can often be important for an autistic person. A 2017 study referred to this as the tailoring of stimulation; being able to regulate sensory inputs thanks to a reduction of stress and anxiety, brought upon by virtue of the environment itself. These safe spaces aren't just conducive for wellbeing, but with the easing of overall stimuli they become a haven for other attributes to blossom. A person's focus increases when in nature, thus providing an opportunity for learning experiences and collaborative activities to be more effective. This can enable the use of skills such as communication, teamwork and problem-solving. If only this was where all teaching and learning took place.

Regarding sensory stimuli, it's common for autistic people to experience some kind of difficulty with the processing of sensory information. This means that any of their senses can be under- or oversensitive, which can also fluctuate and change. You may know, or have seen someone, who wears ear defenders, and this is most likely due to an oversensitivity to noise. Or you may have come across a similar scenario with people who struggle with the feel of certain textures, such as specific foods or clothing. Too much sensory information can trigger certain responses in autistic people, such as meltdown, shutdown and even physical pain. This is usually known as sensory overload. A 2019 journal article found that being outdoors can help autistic people to regulate their senses, repeatedly using the word 'calm' to describe natural environments. Alister Harman strongly relates to this, stating that being outside makes him feel calmer, and adding that he prefers natural light and uncrowded spaces as they're far less stimulating. However, one piece of research from 2023 was resoundingly clear: the environment must be interesting enough to stimulate the senses, but not 'too interesting' so that it becomes overstimulating in any way.

I can deeply relate to this. The natural world buzzes with life and wonder, but is often devoid of human activity, which is what I mostly want to escape from. The wilder, the better. We all know that society can be judgemental. I came across an article from 2020 referring to the natural world being a 'non-judgemental' environment. I love this. It really is a place where we can be feral and visceral if we want to be, but most importantly, we can be ourselves. Alister describes nature as an 'honest' environment. In contrast, he says that many people have what he calls a 'lax relationship with honesty and truth'. Nature does not. I also spoke to Alex Harding, an outdoor learning coordinator from Essex, who echoes these sentiments. Alex works with a range of young people in various outdoor contexts, including school gardening and a holiday nature group. He's very clear that nature doesn't judge, nature doesn't tell children off, and that nature forgives. These are powerful words, from someone who regularly sees nature's positive impacts. While in nature, especially when away from school, children are free. They have less inhibition, and because nature won't look down on them, they are free to be free.

This freedom can rub off on anyone. I have noticed, after many years of working with young people with SEND in outdoor contexts, that when you're with them away from the traditional learning space, they change. I don't mean this in an ominous way. The pressure and containment of the traditional learning environment disappears. The hierarchical structures that exist inside the classroom seem to evaporate, as comfort zones are abandoned, and other strengths get an opportunity to shine. At various stages of my career, I've found myself working with some incredibly challenging children, who have had minimal exposure to outdoor activity and to nature throughout their lives. I've seen some incredible moments. From a teenage boy who'd been excluded from school rescuing a red admiral butterfly, to many of my pupils, across a variety of settings, seeking me out whenever they find a moth so that I can identify it for them. I've also seen tenderness, where the 'cool' kid works collaboratively with those they would usually ignore, and worse, belittle. Observing and guiding them to work together is such a privilege. It's a privilege I don't think I'd get in any other context. Especially without the catalyst that is the natural world.

The 'dys's' are a funny one. By virtue of their definition, they're specific learning difficulties, so generally relate to indoor learning environments, not outdoor ones. As with all neurodivergent conditions, the dys's cause additional mental and emotional strain, through the need for coping and masking, and having to push through the barriers they create for the individual. This means, as with all neurodivergence, that there's an increased risk of poor mental health, and therefore the therapeutic and regulatory aspects of being and working outdoors are obviously beneficial. It's unsurprising that most of the people I spoke to with a diagnosis of one or more of the dys's couldn't articulate specifically why the outdoors was of benefit to them. Those that did leant on the sensory or regulatory aspects of their comorbidities. I'm not saying there aren't any benefits for individuals with one or more of the dys's, but that nature, being non-judgemental, calm and predictable, will generally have a positive effect on anyone who struggles to navigate society.

So, to be of actual benefit to us, people who are neurodivergent are seeking environments that strike a delicate sensory balance, with enough going on in them to pique our interest and stimulate the senses, but not so much as to send them into overdrive – as can often be the case in urban and indoor places. Michael Howard, an autistic countryside ranger for the National Trust in East Sussex, has a strong perspective on this. For him, artificial surroundings aren't enjoyable places to be, and one of the things he does to cope with them is to wear earplugs or headphones. This is a common strategy for people who have sensitivity to sound; particularly those who are autistic. Michael describes himself as being hyper-sensitive to sound and finds most human noise annoying, unbearable, and sometimes even painful. He never experiences those feelings when he is outdoors and only hears the sounds of nature. He is also a professional musician, and a favourite activity for both him and me is to find a peaceful place to just sit down and listen to bird sounds; sometimes known as a sit spot. He also enjoys making field recordings of natural sounds, which he listens to at home for relaxation. Taking the outside inside, in sonic form.

On the day I wrote this section, I went to get my hair cut, and on the drive back I took a detour down some country lanes, just so I could see some greenery. Yes, I suddenly felt an immovable urge to look at a hedge. Why? Because it's calming, and it looks good! Nature is full of colours, but they don't have to be vivid to contrast with the uniform greyness present in so many of our urban environments. Look closely at the pavement below you as you stroll through a city, and you'll soon see that plants such as annual meadowgrass and procumbent pearlwort are growing in the cracks. Green against grey. A microcosmic world amongst the concrete. As Michael says, and I wholeheartedly agree with him, focusing on the details and textures of nature can transport you from the hectic and confusing reality of the everyday to a world that many people never witness. He describes this as a more manageable, logical and simple place to be. He's right. The visual aspects of the natural world appeal to so many people, but perhaps we focus too much on recording its wonder, rather than actually immersing ourselves in it.

I asked Alice Armstrong, one of the founders of the Conservation Equity Project (CEP), why she thinks nature is good for her neurodivergent brain. She made an interesting point, that growing up in London made her connection to the outdoors stronger, making those moments she spends in nature feel especially sacred. Michael's view echoed this and added more depth from a sensory autistic perspective. He thinks that urban areas can be confusing and overwhelming places for neurodivergent people. Why? Michael listed some of the reasons: lots of people, noise, unpleasant smells and erratic movement. He doesn't think there can be a starker contrast with this than being in your favourite natural place on your own or with a good – and quiet – friend, experiencing nature with all your senses. If the colours and light become too much, he said, you just close your eyes, and concentrate more intently on sounds. If there's an unpleasant smell, you can move a few metres until it's gone. You are in control, in a way you can't possibly be in a manmade environment. I've never thought about it like that before.

Both Michael, and Larissa Cooper (an autistic and ADHD ecologist from Norfolk) use the term 'grounding' to describe how they feel themselves, and other neurodivergent folk, benefit from nature. I like this term.

It came up a lot when I went to some free mindfulness sessions through my local mental health service, and I use it in a lot of my outdoor teaching. In basic terms, it's when you refocus your attention on the physical world around you, to reconnect with the present. Grounding, in a natural environment, is more than just focusing, it's a fully immersive experience. Sometimes I stand in a natural environment and as I process the range of information flooding over me, it results in instances of euphoria. Walk down a woodland path after a springtime rain shower, carpets of bluebells either side of you, as the smell of wet soil and grass cloys in your nostrils, and you've got all the ingredients for a sensory buffet. Larissa says that being outside feels innate to us and where we should be. For her it isn't overstimulating at all and has the opposite effect, resetting her, as a restorative environment should do.

It took me ages, but I eventually found the right person to help me explain the benefits of nature connection from more of a medical perspective. That person is Helen Mason. Helen is an occupational therapist, a sensory integration practitioner and an eye movement desensitization and reprocessing (EMDR) therapist from Devon. As well as working part-time for the NHS, she also works part-time as founder and co-director of Rise and Rewild Community Interest Company, which provides 'integrative medicine and nature-based therapies for the community'. Her own connection with nature began as a child, playing on her best friend's parents' farm. She grew up running around the fields, dressing up as a fairy in the farmhouse garden and messing about on the hay bales, the latter of which were off-limits. She appreciates the irony that the place she felt most safe and free as a child was also one of the most dangerous places you can be; working farms deserve respect. To this day she treasures the crucial early nature connections she made through outdoor play.

Helen also enthuses about the sensory experiences of the outdoors as a neurodivergent young person. The freedom of the fields, the cool water of the brook running over her feet, moss moving with the water and the bubbling soundscape behind it all. It was a release, and the opposite of the discomfort and shame she was experiencing in the classroom at the time. Helen is dyslexic, and would avidly try to conform to expectations, but would frequently fail. At primary school, a teacher had once made her stand at the front of her class and lift her dress up to prove she wasn't cheating in a spelling test. The shame of this still haunts her today. She did cheat, but it was to mitigate not being able to visually process what she was copying down. The irony of this is that her 'cheat sheets' were always incorrect, anyway. Her escape became the arts, which gave her ways to express herself and to survive the effort she was putting in just to keep up with her peers. She also had the sea nearby, and spent hours sitting in beach caves playing didgeridoo with her friends, the pulsing echoes and rhythms creating ritual moments and mutual memories.

This all feeds into why she became an occupational therapist. Occupational therapy was an approach brought to the UK in the 1930s by Dr Elizabeth Casson, who had a firm belief in the healing potential of meaningful, purpose-driven activities to support the recovery of soldiers experiencing shellshock. In this context, 'occupation' is any meaningful activity. Anything you do, from brushing your teeth, to playing a musical instrument, can be seen through the lens of occupation, and therefore, has the potential to support recovery. Occupational therapy has always put people at its core, and recognises the differences in meaningful activities for each person. It isn't a surprise, given her own nature connection, that throughout her career as an occupational therapist Helen has had a specific interest in the relational, co-regulating use of nature as a therapeutic tool, or co-therapist. We can even view connection with nature as an occupation, made up of a wide range of meaningful activities stimulating all the senses. Although Helen believes that new technologies like AI will transform the health sector in ways we can't currently imagine, she finds herself drawn back to working in simple ways, approaches that are grounded to the earth and planet, and focus on connecting with nature.

I asked her for some examples, and she had plenty. Twenty years ago, when working in young people's mental health services, she made a vegetable garden with one of the cleaners. This was before the guerrilla-gardening movement had a resurgence, but was still pushing against boundaries. Basically, they were digging out a bed with the young people behind the unit, with the unit manager initially turning a blind eye. More recently, a similar guerrilla experience saw the miraculous creation of a flower bed on another NHS unit where she was working. She describes how, after finishing a therapy session, she would offer young people the option of going out to dig in the flower bed. They would mash up written trauma narratives, destroying the paper until it was a pulp. This would give the young person proprioceptive (our ability to perceive the location and movements of our body parts) and vestibular (our sense of space and balance) movement and feedback, while symbolically transforming their trauma into something new and life-affirming. They would then physically bury the pulp in the ground so it could be held there, not go home with it. The nurturing of the bed was a source of comfort, reflection and enjoyment for the staff. They would water it during their lunch breaks, and observe the cultivation process, with it acting as a form of distraction.

Helen's company, Rise and Rewild, operates out of Powderham Castle in Devon. Prior to and during the Covid pandemic, she took frequent walks through the castle grounds with colleagues from the health sector who were experiencing burnout. The peaceful surroundings were a contrast to the intense sensory experiences found in medical settings. When the pandemic hit, she found that these walks were becoming increasingly vital, and she began to question the traditional thinking that therapy should be done sitting indoors in a psychosocial vacuum. The combination of walking and talking, alongside the unpredictable offerings of the natural world as a co-regulator, offer her such deep symbolism that she continues to find it endlessly fascinating. She began to practice forest bathing, applying her training in sensory integration therapy, and her knowledge of the natural world, to be able to immerse others in the sensory wonder of the outdoors. It harked back to her own childhood: the bubbling brook, the moss on the water, the freedom of the fields. She can facilitate these experiences for other people through her therapeutic outdoor work, and the possibilities for connection, sensory integration and feelings of safety are endless.

As Helen says, there's something truly magical about watching a seed germinate and grow. It is to nurture and witness creation and growth from nothing. There's an abundance of metaphor here. Roots. Branches. Blooming. Neurodivergent people spend much of their lives trying to blossom in the hardest of environments.

To be able to reconnect with nature and, as Helen says, use it as a co-regulator, is for us to come full circle. It's all a bit too profound for my ADHD brain to process! I wonder how much of this is innate. I read some interesting 2024 research suggesting that people with ADHD tend to *explore* an environment when foraging for resources, rather than automatically exploiting it, which they see as an adaptive advantage in certain settings. If neurodivergence has always been part of humanity, I do wonder if, when we were hunter-gatherers, the different strengths and skills of neurodivergent people made them a favourable component of any unit. Now, with how we communicate and perceive things, especially through technology, have we cast this advantage aside? Perhaps this innate desire to be outdoors and connect with it harks all the way back to these instincts from pre-modern times.

If you think about it, many outdoor jobs feature tasks that involve collecting, organising and utilising natural resources. Perhaps many neurodivergent people are drawn to working outside because they can use these skills, which may now be seen as less desirable in the artificial world we've made for ourselves. Perhaps we subconsciously find our way back to a way of being that embraces our differences and is part of our wiring. Ultimately, the benefits of being outdoors are there for everyone, not just neurodivergent people. However, there are clearly patterns and correlations in how many neurodivergent people seemingly 'need' this connection to help them manage a variety of challenges. This may be anxiety, mood, sensory processing, emotional regulation, focus, concentration or just to escape from the trappings of society. We know that the natural world doesn't judge us like the human world does. It allows us to be free, and to be ourselves. It's such a simple, effective and free resource that we can utilise for wellbeing. With all this in mind, is it any surprise that so many neurodivergent people work outdoors and in roles focusing on nature and the environment? It's time to explore this in a little more depth.

CHAPTER FIVE

More than just the saviour of the orangutan

The conservation sector

The original focus of this book was to connect neurodivergence with a mythical realm that I kept referring to as the environmental sector. The best way to introduce this was with a definition, and that was where my issues began. 'Environmental' literally means all that is 'connected with the natural conditions in which people, animals and plants live'. If you consider this in the broadest sense, that means everything, right? Not only is it all-encompassing, but also the natural conditions that the definition describes are as complex and interwoven as the jobs I was researching. I kept telling myself that I had to sort these out and made a futile attempt to start listing and categorising them. One source would outline a tonne of jobs, but another would throw a complete curveball at me, saying, 'Joe, nuclear energy is a green job, you'll have to cover that as well', and my head was spinning all over the place trying to make sense of it all. Help came unexpectedly, when a friend did the kind thing and told me that the term 'environmental' is confusing, and kind of means anything and everything. Listening to them was my lightbulb moment.

You see, they were right, and the answer was always there, staring back at me from the groupings I was trying to create. Conservation. Not only had this term arisen in all my research, but it was also the most familiar. When you think about people who work in environmental roles, the default is to tag this as conservation, which means the 'preservation, protection, or restoration of the natural environment and of wildlife'. While, like 'environmental', this is not a narrow label, it brings with it more specificity. More comfort. When I say conservation, the mind conjures visions of elaborate jobs; perhaps a research team trekking in what's left of the Bornean rainforests to find and protect the last orangutans. This is a glamorous and adventurous example; the reality is that anyone can be a conservationist. As well as a sphere of employment, it's also an attitude. A way of being. It's the 'world' that my interests and writing immerse me in, however, I wouldn't claim for a second to be a part of the conservation sector. You can be a punk, but not have a mohawk, tattoos and a leather jacket. It's who you are.

In professional terms, a conservationist works in any role that directly or indirectly conserves wildlife and the natural environment. There are myriad roles available, and they're all interwoven. However, it can be a highly competitive job market. Almost all jobs require you to have a university degree, and it's desirable to have a lot of voluntary experience before undertaking a paid role. The most interesting observation I've made is that although people often gravitate towards working in conservation because they would like to work outside and/or with animals, there seems to be an ever-increasing requirement for people. To conserve the environment, organisations must generate income. This requires people. They must provide education and attempt to facilitate changes in societal habits to safeguard the environment for future generations. These also require people. They must fight on behalf of the environment, lobbying and campaigning at all levels to effect change. People, again. It's fascinating just how reliant the entire concept of conservation is on people; and deeply ironic that we're the ones who put the scars across our natural world in the first place. It's a paradox.

So, what's the framework of the conservation sector and how does it function in the UK? Through political devolution, conservation sits in the hands of the respective governments in England, Scotland, Wales and Northern Ireland. These also carry responsibility for areas of the economy that can have a direct impact on wildlife, such as housing, fisheries, forestry and agriculture. In each of the nations, a statutory body takes the lead on wildlife conservation. For example, in England you may be familiar with the work of, or have heard the name of Natural England, the government body responsible for English wildlife. Between 1973 and 1991, this was the remit of the Nature Conservancy Council, a government agency that oversaw the designation and management of national nature reserves and conservation areas. Upon its breakup, it was split into three statutory bodies: Scottish Natural Heritage (now known as NatureScot), the Countryside Council for Wales, and English Nature. This process also saw the formation of a public body, known as the Joint Nature Conservation Committee. This group is made up of members from the national bodies, along with independent members, under a chairperson, and serves to advise on strategic nature conservation and organisational issues across all four of the UK nations' statutory conservation bodies.

Conservation organisations and employers work across various spheres. There are charitable organisations, businesses, academic organisations and lots of governmental organisations. Many of the employers in conservation are household names. The charitable ones are the most recognisable; it's likely you'll have heard of both the National Trust and the Wildlife Trusts. These often get put together under the moniker 'NGOs' – non-governmental organisations. Governmental organisations are also easily recognisable. You'll most likely have heard of the Environment Agency, for example. Organisational structures in conservation are almost like miniature ecosystems themselves, demonstrating the symbiotic relationship between society, these organisations, and the natural environments they strive to protect. Roles interweave – take a nature reserve, for example. You can't have one without people to manage it, both in terms of practical conservation and visitor experiences; especially in those larger flagship reserves, like RSPB Minsmere in Suffolk, that pride themselves on the interactions they are able to offer. This diversification towards connecting nature and culture serves a dual purpose. As well as creating alternative income streams, walks, talks or children's trails, for example, open these natural environments to new audiences, once again demonstrating increasing focus upon people in the conservation sector.

I want to start by discussing those at the frontline of UK conservation. Whether they're bashing bracken, fixing fenceposts, coppicing trees or whatever other tasks their roles might entail, their careers in practical conservation will always have variety. The most recognisable role of this type is that of the ranger. We've already met Alister Harman – he's a National Trust ranger at Lyme Park on the north-western tip of the Peak District National Park. He describes his role as requiring him to be a 'jack of all trades and master of a few others'. His day-to-day work involves following a site management plan outlining the tasks to be done. It could be attending to a broken fence or a fallen tree, and isn't prescriptive at all. He uses a great analogy from a fellow ranger. Their job is a lot like juggling, with the various balls being their different responsibilities: habitat management, visitor management, incident response, volunteer management, health and safety, surveying and site maintenance, to name a few. The trick is to give each of those balls the appropriate amount of attention so that you don't drop them.

Alister mentions surveying, which is an integral component of conservation work. Ecologist Larissa Cooper also does a lot of freelance ecological surveying and says that without it, we don't see changes and understand species' behaviours and nuances. She adds that we need surveying to inform conservation efforts, or we could end up negatively impacting species and habitats. The world is changing, and those who conduct survey work are often the first to notice these changes. Ecology is the study of organisms and their interactions with their surrounding environments, and some other specific tasks an ecologist might undertake include environmental impact assessments and other fieldwork. I liked the way Larissa described things, so I asked her how she would describe the role of an ecologist. 'It's the person standing up for nature through monitoring and understanding the interactions of species in their environment; and making recommendations with groundings in evidence', she said. Ecologists usually specialise in a specific area, such as freshwater, or flora; she specialises in botanical and habitat surveys, and bat emergence and activity surveys. Obviously, this means working at night and driving to a location before sunset to set up her kit (bat detector and night vision camera) ready to watch for emerging bats.

Larissa absolutely loves being an ecologist. She described a magical moment where she almost came face to face with a barbastelle bat, which flew into a barn mid-survey before positioning itself in a gap in the doorway. Around two hours after sunset, she packs up and drives home, describing the whole process as possibly the most relaxing job she's ever done. In fact, she can't imagine herself ever working in anything other than ecology and loves the variation it brings. The most diverse elements of her role are the locations that she visits, which are often places she would never get to see otherwise. Beautiful houses, estates and farms. Derelict buildings and industrial complexes. Celebrities' countryside houses. A solar farm with a flock of sheep running around her all night. A derelict pig farm, looking (and feeling) like the perfect setting for a horror movie. I understood the aesthetic side and the sense of place, but found myself wondering how autistic ecologists cope with the lottery of where they might be working. Dedication to a single site can forge a deep relationship and connection with the land, but surely there's an impact if the location is constantly changing.

I got some insight into this from autistic ecologist Naomi Davis, whose favourite thing about their job is that they get to find and categorise things. They love the fact that every day in their job is different; despite the daily tasks being the same, the locations vary so much, and it is their responsibility to record the variations in species that occur. Like Larissa's, their work is highly seasonal, and in the summer months they might be out in the field 80 per cent of the time, undertaking surveys all over Wales. They also conduct large-scale habitat work, where they turn up on site and use all the surrounding sensory input to build a picture of the environment and infer what plants or animals could be present. Naomi described a process where their brain is 'on' all the time, and they are able to extract and store information that matters. This might be a list of birds, by sound, and a list of plants, from visuals. They're always actively looking out for signs of mammals, like badger setts or latrines. You might think that such a high level of sensory stimulation would eventually cause overwhelm, but this isn't the case for Naomi.

Colin Everett is a very different type of surveyor. He works as a consultant ornithologist, conducting fieldwork for environmental impact assessments, which then accompany applications for wind turbine developments. Basically, he gets a salary to do some hardcore birdwatching, which, for a birder, is the stuff of dreams. An assignment usually lasts for two years, and in this time a variety of habitat and species surveys must take place. A key feature of Colin's work is a vantage point (VP) survey, which is an older, but industry-standard method of gathering data on the potential collision risk for key bird species (especially raptors, waders and larger wildfowl). He demonstrated to me, with some wonderfully scenic photos to help build an image, that VPs must be in 1–10 (or more, depending on the site size) pre-chosen locations around the prospective wind farm site, and overlap so that the whole of the area can be seen. For the best visual coverage, VPs are generally on higher open ground where the observer (Colin) surveys a 2km semi-circular area, in front of and either side of them. It sounds awesome. Timings operate in a cycle, with a requirement of 72 survey hours per VP, evenly spread across the year.

I told Colin that most people with an interest in wildlife would be jealous. He acknowledged this, but also bemoaned the fact that it isn't so much fun in winter, especially as he feels the cold and sometimes needs to wear seven or eight layers to keep it out. I asked if he could move about, but he said that he can't during the actual act of surveying, because he must be alert to what's around him, which makes sense. This means he sees more. He may be surveying birds, but he also encounters an array of other wildlife, and shared some incredible pictures with me. There are seven images of birds' nests, which he took during surveys using best-practice guidelines. They feature reed bunting, goldfinch, chaffinch, linnet, common snipe, curlew and golden plover. These are significant records. Two are on the Red list of birds of conservation concern, and another two are on the Amber list. There's the astonishing scene of a cuckoo chick in a meadow pipit nest, a gorgeous stoat, and a plethora of lepidoptera. In terms of human interaction, surveying can be a lonely job, which suits Colin perfectly, but he's never far from some wild companions.

Most conservation organisations, particularly those who are charities, will offer some form of environmental education as part of their charitable objectives. What I like about the range of approaches on offer across the sector is that there really is something for everyone. There are loads of high-quality downloadable resources available. Some come as sequential units of work, and many come with lesson plans. Organisations that manage their own nature reserves will almost certainly have at least one site that schools can visit. Such excursions offer an opportunity for young people to enthuse about wildlife, and for them to engage them with a variety of practical learning experiences that they may not otherwise have. Some organisations employ specific education teams, who work on linking their provisions with the national curriculum to enhance their attraction to schools. Some offer outreach: I remember arranging for the Norfolk Wildlife Trust to visit a pupil referral unit I was working in. They brought in a box of barn owl pellets to dissect, and the students loved differentiating between the various partial rodent skulls found within them. These educational opportunities are not exclusive to schools, and all visitable sites are likely to have an event calendar, which is open to everyone.

We mustn't forget the importance of engaging the next generation with nature. A lot of work happens under the guise of youth engagement, but meaningful positive outcomes are still a long way off. I know from years of teaching in a nature-rich county that there is a real danger of young people disconnecting from the outside world. It's brilliant to have lots of free resources at your disposal, but if the delivery of the content is flat and uninspiring, will we really inspire our youth to leave their online bubbles to look at some wildflowers? We often think of social media as the antithesis of the natural world, but there're some influencers who strive to connect young people with nature, such as Lira Valencia. Lira, who refers to herself as the David Attenborough of Croydon, shows that nature can be much more accessible to hard-to-reach groups of young people if it is presented by people that they resonate with, who relate to their struggles, and who sound like them. I'm deeply passionate about inclusion and an equity of access and opportunity, and I truly believe that effective role-modelling is the key to this.

Beyond statutory education, we must have people who can teach, train, and inspire the next generation of conservationists, although the disconnect between the primary and secondary phases of education when it comes to the natural sciences is vast. Many roles in the conservation sector require a degree, alongside significant practical experience. However, to achieve a degree, the courses and their facilitators must be available in the first place. I spoke to Dr Steve Allain, a lecturer in zoology, who has diagnoses of both autism and ADHD. He undertook his own degree in zoology at Anglia Ruskin University in Cambridge, and now lectures at a university in the same group, but in

Essex. Steve always knew he'd need as many hours of practical experience under his belt as possible, so he began involving himself with local groups. He found himself working multiple jobs in the hospitality sector, alongside research and studying, to make ends meet. Eventually, he earned a doctorate in biodiversity management from the University of Kent, and was considering becoming a lecturer. However, after countless rejections due to his lack of post-doctoral experience, he began to consider other roles in the conservation sector.

All was not lost. Thanks to his great reputation and growing bank of published work, his mentors at Cambridge put him forward for a lecturing role and he began working a few hours a week. Eventually, when a full-time position arose, his colleagues told him he should apply, and he was successful. He is now lecturing both degree- and master's-level animal science students, on a full-time basis. Although he enjoys it, he says he's still got a lot to grasp, but hopes that his passion and enthusiasm come across in the lectures he delivers. Being a neurodivergent lecturer comes with its challenges, though. Steve says that he can be quite gung-ho in the way he works and can clash with authority, but gets positive results, and is building a mutually respectful relationship. This year he's been supervising several master's students and a degree student, the latter of whom has been researching frog genetics, which is an area Steve works in himself. He loves accelerating the passion, and hopefully the careers, of his students. Ultimately, it's exciting to be playing such an important role in developing the next generation of conservation professionals, isn't it?

There are also the people on the receiving end of lectures. Those studying zoology, conservation, ecology and so much more, in further and higher education. Şeniz

Mustafa is studying for a master's degree in ecology and conservation in Brighton. She also has dyslexia, autism and ADHD. Alongside researching bird vomit, she also runs events for her university ecological society and volunteers for conservation organisations. Her day-to-day life may involve lectures and writing, but her studies also utilise placements and visits. Şeniz enjoys the outdoor and practical elements of her course, as lectures can be very routine, but she also thrives on regularity, something she attributes to her autism. Sitting in a lecture isn't quite the same, she said, as going outside and identifying beetles. I spoke to other students, all of whom were undertaking astonishing amounts of volunteer work, as they already knew how important this would be when they came to apply for entry-level roles. Some told me of their wondrous placements, all over the world, with animals most of us will never encounter, but the barriers and burnout that accompany these were also all too real.

It's not just education and engagement that inspires the next generation. A lot of time, money and effort is put into the messages we receive from conservation organisations. I spoke to quite a few people who work in what is known as 'sci-comm', a relatively new term, short for science-communication, whereby science and society connect via social media. One of these people is Stephanie Martin, who describes herself as a freelance environmental communicator. She is also dyslexic. Her main area of work is green marketing, where she helps eco-conscious businesses and people who love nature to expand their presence online through social media management, web design, and brand development. Alongside this, she also does some podcasting, live presenting, social media content creation and writing. Does she love it? Of course she does. There's so much variety, and she gets to control what she does and when. It's a creative job, but also involves strategy, data analysis and research. Mostly she loves communicating about the natural world and how important and special it is, with the goal of inspiring other people to want to protect it in any way they can.

Does being dyslexic hold her back? No, but it's the main reason she works freelance now. Stephanie feels that throughout her education, volunteering and work, people often wouldn't have believed her if she told them she was struggling with something due to her dyslexia. She thinks that sometimes people have an idea in their head of what a dyslexic person should be like, and it isn't her. They don't expect someone with dyslexia to be a writer and an editor, or to have science degrees, and Stephanie says that they are wrong for thinking this. It's not so much the lack of understanding, but more the lack of belief that frustrates her. Freelance work removes this barrier entirely. She is, she says, the best boss she has ever had. In fact, as she reflects, being dyslexic is probably the biggest factor in steering her career into sci-comms. She loves her dyslexic brain, with its wiring toward creativity, storytelling and curiosity. Now, all she wants to do is communicate her passion for nature as creatively as possible, particularly through stories. So much so that she's currently studying for the UK gold-standard journalism qualification thanks to a bursary from the Journalism Diversity Fund.

Big conservation organisations often have big causes and even bigger messages that they want to share. They weave together their own networks of communication, condensing and sharing information with the wider public to promote engagement. I spoke with Lucy McRobert, who isn't neurodivergent herself, but I know she has significant experience in the conservation sector through various communication roles. This includes working for the Wildlife Trusts, as a researcher for writers Tony Juniper and Stephen Moss, as a writer for both Plantlife International and BirdLife International, and for the Sound Approach, an organisation that works on understanding birdsong. Lucy described communications staff as 'the melting pot that holds everything together', yet conservation colleagues can often perceive them as an unnecessary luxury item, lacking in skills. Ultimately, though, effective communication in this sector requires many skills and an overarching knowledge of multiple conservation areas. What does a 'comms' person do then? Lucy said it depends on the size of the organisation. In larger ones, you might specialise in a particular area like copywriting, digital communications, or media. At smaller ones, you basically have to know an awful lot about an awful lot. Not to mention the everchanging (almost weekly) landscape of technologies, platforms, and channels.

As Lucy so succinctly put it, communications work in any field is essentially a translation service, taking complex technical issues and distilling them into an accessible format for a more general audience. Within that audience are multiple sub-audiences, which you must deeply understand – what makes them tick, what their values are and what will motivate them – if you want to infiltrate and spread a message. It seems like a branch of psychology to me, and being someone with minimal knowledge of how all this works, the level of insight that goes into it astounded me. She distilled it for me, saying that there's no point being on TikTok if you're running a legacy campaign targeting older audiences. It sounds like a great career path though, especially if you like variety in your role. Lucy said that when she was working at a large

NGO, no two days were the same, and could feature anything from planning engagement campaigns and writing articles to editing magazines and attending seemingly endless meetings. Whatever the level of organisation, communications tasks are eclectic and include scheduling social media content, updating websites, design work and uniting with colleagues to work on key messages.

For these organisations to have a message, they need to have leadership, and I wondered what it's like to work in the higher echelons of the sector, so I asked Adam Taylor, CEO of Gwent Wildlife Trust, who has diagnoses of both autism and ADHD. Adam told me that leading teams in the conservation charity sector is a huge privilege, as everyone you work with cares so deeply about the issues we're facing that they've chosen to dedicate their careers or volunteer their time, to solve them, which makes for great colleagues, and energising, exciting workplaces. He said that as charities have delivery of their mission and serving the community at their heart, they are often organised in a more ground-up than top-down fashion, and use approaches like community development and outreach to understand issues on the ground before co-developing solutions. As a result of this, leadership in the sector is very democratic, non-hierarchical, and all about listening, learning and discussing possibilities, which often means the person leading on a solution is not the most senior person in the room, but the person with the best ideas because of their unique experiences and expertise.

In Adam's experience, this non-hierarchical environment means that mostly, the best ideas win out. This culture helps Adam, and other individuals from diverse backgrounds, to feel genuinely welcomed and included.

He is hopeful that recognition of the significant impacts these working environments are delivering will increase their use in other settings to drive equality, diversity and inclusion (EDI) more widely, particularly with regard to neurodivergence. To my knowledge, this best EDI practice, exemplified by organisations in the conservation sector, hasn't been described in the same place before, and I hope that people will take inspiration from it and adapt their own workplaces and practices. Adam underplays it, but the benefits of having neurodivergent senior leaders in any organisation are limitless, not only as an ally for other neurodivergent colleagues, but also as a driver for change.

Of course, all the above examples are merely a snapshot of the jobs available in the conservation sector; an introduction for those of us outside it. Simply put, the diversity of roles in the conservation sector reflects nature's own biodiversity and abundance.

Finally, I spoke to Kerryn Humphreys, the editor of the Countryside Jobs Service (CJS) website. Kerryn is also autistic. The CJS bills itself as 'an ethical business working in harmony with environmental professionals to conserve the British countryside and natural world'. I asked Kerryn about how much change the CJS has seen across the sector. She said that in the 30 years since its inception, the CJS has seen seismic shifts in the types of jobs available across the countryside and conservation sectors, but the purpose of these jobs remains unchanged: to make the countryside a better place through conserving nature, increasing biodiversity, protecting landscapes, making green (and blue) spaces more accessible, and informing people of the connections between all of these. Kerryn said that back in 1994, when the first printed CJS edition came out, ecology was a fledgling area of the sector. Now it's understood to be a vital part of the industry, and is one of the main areas of work, along with the practical management and conservation roles. She described the conservation sector as I have; vast and sprawling, with as much variety as the countryside itself.

Kerryn shared some jobs that stuck in her mind because they were so bizarre, for example, a 'flying shepherd' for a wildlife trust, which wasn't quite the helicopter stock-handling job the CJS were imagining, but caring for a flock of rare breed sheep grazing across a series of nature reserves and moving them to new pastures. The 'flying' was in reference to a 'flying flock'. She mused about the many jobs where you must be comfortable in your own company, as you'd be the only person living on a lonely peninsula or island reserve, or where you must have your own dog, for tracking and companionship. Work in conservation is always going to require a unique skillset, but what if these distinct abilities were innate, and built into your cognitive wiring? What if they came alongside a set of behaviours that stood you apart from your peers positively in certain areas, yet, at the same time, singled you out as different in ways that many other people couldn't understand? This is what we bring as neurodivergent folk, and the narrative around us has been negative for far too long, so let's celebrate these strengths, skills and successes together.

CHAPTER SIX

Out of the box and into the holographic forest

Strengths

One of the more recent narratives around neurodivergence is that it's some kind of superpower. I don't personally find ADHD super, or a power. At best, I might be able to juggle multiple projects and ideas at once. I say 'juggle'; what I mean is that I can start these things and then struggle to ever finish them. I don't feel like the symptoms I experience are helpful or conducive to wellbeing and peak performance at work. However, many people I've spoken to for this book believe that their diagnoses bring a plethora of strengths and positives to their working lives. I don't disagree with the sentiment that the differences in neurodivergent people's brains mean that we can offer additionality in certain areas of work. However, I line manage a diverse range of people and believe that everyone has the potential to shine, neurodivergent or not. I read a piece of research from 2020 raising an interesting point about neurodivergent employees 'resembling thwarted geniuses', so-called diamonds in the rough, but there are also counter-opinions to this; that these types of beliefs have the potential to inadvertently pressurise neurodivergent employees into being exceptional. As well as strengths, there will always be difficulties with any difference.

Research suggests that there are several competencies in which neurodivergent people excel professionally. Creativity is one of these, another is problem-solving.

ADHD can bring something called hyperfocus (a trait whereby attention is narrower and has a tighter focus on 'stimuli of endogenous interest'). Autism can add exquisite memory skills and the acquisition of 'special interests', where someone develops an intense focus on a specific topic. The strengths resulting from a diagnosis in one of the dys's are more subtle, presenting unique verbal, visual and organisational skills, depending on the specific diagnosis. Having read an awful lot about this and after speaking to a wide range of people for this book, these were certainly recurrent themes in my own research. In fact, when considering the question of whether their neurodivergence brings any specific strengths to their work, most of the people I spoke with began their answer by stating that they feel like they 'think differently'. Usually this coalesced into a narrative of being able to approach problem-solving from angles that others may not, as a direct impact of their brains processing things differently. That's part of the beauty of neurodivergence. We just need to harness these unconventional perspectives and remember that it's our society that has made them appear unconventional in the first place.

Hazel Jackson of the Woodland Trust described this as being able to see obvious connections and join dots much more quickly than other people. To her, these are the things that appear most logically. Whilst she's certain this is a strength, she also noted how frustrating it can be when she's ahead of people and then has to try and get them to follow her way of thinking. She referred to this as 'big ideas thinking' and shared how she has had to adapt herself to utilise this approach. She prioritises what she can recognise as game-changing and identifies who to influence to make change happen. Once this process begins, she can delegate to her team, as she trusts them to go forward with her ideas. I love this; it's what leaders may recognise as an implementation cycle, but I view it as a flowchart of thought that Hazel's brain follows. She will, however, move on to the next idea immediately in a flurry of energy, and if an idea doesn't follow through, then the energy can collapse into low mood, demotivation and flatness.

When I asked Emily Clarke of Binnies about her strengths, she immediately raised this notion of being able to think differently. In fact, she feels that she sees things differently to (pretty much) everyone else, and calls this 'lateral thinking'. She also described herself as a 'super empath', which is a highly sensitive person who tunes into the emotions and energies of others, often experiencing these feelings themselves on a deep emotional level. Is this always a strength? Emily accepts it can be tough to always lead with emotion, but it does mean that she develops strong and meaningful connections with people she works with, which can obviously be advantageous in a team or leadership environment. I suggested that this might make her vulnerable, as other people may recognise and exploit her kindness. She has experience of this at a previous employer, who led her into a meeting to take her off a huge project, with no warning or feedback. The experience has given her more resilience and enabled her to grow professionally, but it left a bitter impression.

Lottie Trewick gave it yet another name, calling it 'out of the box' thinking. What did she mean? Well, it's like having an ability to piece things together in ways she finds other people can't; a similar notion to those of Hazel and Emily. My ears pricked up when Lottie said that she's also great at communicating ideas to others through turning them into stories. She added that she's able to make things more 'interesting and exciting', but I offered another angle on this. With my professional hat on, I think that due to her dyslexia, she struggles to process certain information, and, therefore, automatically distils it for other people in a way that she knows she can access it herself. She's basically making a societal adjustment for others because of how she's had to adjust for them; it's crazy, really. She thought about this and then reflected that, yes, her brain enables her to be creative in how she thinks, whilst also loving logic and science. They don't always work in unison though, and so she must, 'do science, but do it creatively'. I can't think of a better way for me to digest scientific stuff – she's spot-on.

Alister, as eloquent as every answer he's given me, described what seems to be a practically limitless ability to hyperfocus, or drill down on whatever he's doing. Hyperfocus is a term that occurs in most modern narratives about ADHD and autism, especially in the social media generation. Neurodivergent people are more likely to focus on interests that drive an internal goal, rather than a sensory need or response. The current narrative is that hyperfocus is a superpower, and some people describe it as a complete dissociation from the surrounding environment. Of course, if someone can utilise it effectively, they can smash out important pieces of work, projects, and such, but as hyperfocus involves fixating on something of interest, what is that at the detriment of? There are drawbacks. Sustaining a high level of attention can be physically and mentally exhausting. Focusing so much on one thing can result in others being left behind, like an important meeting, interpersonal relationships, or even one's own self-care needs.

Larissa Cooper is another person who considers hyperfocus to be one of their key strengths, especially as it means she can learn new skills relatively quickly. She described how, during the Covid lockdown, she was able to teach herself to weave textiles on a multi-shaft loom through hyperfocusing on it. Now, her current hyperfocuses are biodiversity net gain and bat ecology. I can see how, when you work in the field of ecology, being able to learn everything you can about a topic must be beneficial to the role, especially when surveying. Colin Everett talked about his experience with hyperfocus in another way, but also one which must be advantageous in his job. He described his main strength as his 'desire and ability to focus and concentrate on apparently small details.' He's so adept at this, he's certain this is one of the main reasons people employ him. Often when out in the field he will amaze people with his ability to notice everything. Even if someone else is talking, if there's a fragment of a bird call somewhere in the distance, he will pick it up, and usually identify it as well.

This is something that Naomi concurs with. They say that their 'brain is always on, and they get to use their super senses.' As it does for Colin, this often means hearing things that other people can't. They use a bat detector during surveys but can also, astonishingly, hear bats echolocating. They say that they know almost every birdsong and call, even a tiny 'peep' doesn't slip the radar. It's visual, too. They can see things people can't, like the path of a polecat through long grass. Combining this with a bit of hyperfocus, they say that they're always watching, so can find bird nests quickly by observing the parents around the nest. Naomi can call upon powers usually absent in humans like the

Marshal Bravestarr of the ecology world (proper niche reference, there), but constantly being in this state of awareness must be draining. It's a prime example of the paradox I mentioned earlier: escaping the sensory stimulation of urban environments by immersing ourselves in nature, which, to them, is also stimulating, just not in a negative way. As Naomi acknowledges, at work this hyperesthesia (a fancy word for heightening of the senses) is awesome, but in many other situations it can make their life very difficult.

I asked how Naomi coped with this, and they said that although natural sounds can fill up their sensory bucket, it never quite overflows. In fact, the only time they've ever come close to overwhelm is when they've been listening to the dawn chorus. I've never thought about the growing crescendo and layering of the dawn chorus, and how that must feel for anyone with difficulties in sensory processing. Naomi is clear that this is due to their ability to process and name every bird they hear, rather than the pressure of processing the sounds themselves. The fact that this is manageable shows that Naomi must be able to process lots of input quickly. Alister described a similar ability to do this, particularly when the information is sensorial in nature. He used the example of planning to plant an orchard. He can readily plot out where each tree needs to go, how they'll interact, their ongoing management and how to prepare for success, all in the space of a few minutes. However, although he may be able to conceptualise the entirety of a project, explaining that process to others causes difficulty and takes time.

Alister explained how this process looks for him and told me to imagine a kind of visualisation meditation technique, where you rest with your eyes shut and actively visualise whatever you want to focus on. Now, he said, you must imagine that visualisation as an imprint on the landscape around you. I did it and envisaged a connective blueprint of environmental features, with *Star Trek* vibes, and pop-up visions of holographic forests. It must be so cool to experience the world like this. This got me thinking about fractals – patterns that can be found in nature that self-repeat in different sizes and magnifications. Think of a snowflake or the leaves on a tree, for example. Naomi describes being able to feel the intrinsic links between all natural things, so when they're in a new place, they can almost always tell what will be around them. If X tree species are in Y habitat, they can expect to find A, B, and C. The connections are tangible to them. Many of us don't, or can't, process things in this deeply elemental way. To me, and many others, having the ability to perceive the world in this way feels like more than a strength – it feels magical.

This is also the experience of Joe Bristow. He's a woodland ranger and educator with dyslexia, who I came across quite late in the development of the book. I loved how he described connecting with nature in a visual-spatial sense, saying that his brain thinks in pictures and maps; he can walk around a nature reserve or woodland once, and then the imprint of it is there in his head, like a three-dimensional map. It's a case of instantly knowing where every tree and path should be. He considers this to be a huge strength in his work as a ranger. He's adamant that we need more neurodivergent people harnessing their unique skills to engage other people with nature. He talked of his own struggles to recall the nomenclature of animals, and that what we really require are people who can share the aesthetics, the visuals, with us. He also wants to know the story of the creature, its folklore, and how it fits into the wider ecosystem. He uses the oak tree as an example. One tree nurtures over 20,000 creatures, extending upwards and then deep into the ground. Networks everywhere.

Another trait of autism that's occasionally written about is what's known as 'enhanced pattern recognition'. Studies have found that people with autism tend to perform well in visual tasks, and brain scans have shown them to have an increase of activity in areas of the brain that are responsible for perception and pattern recognition. In principle, this means that people with autism may excel at jobs that involve manipulation and interpretation of numbers and data, in sectors such as computer programming and data analysis. This is exactly the case for Pete Tomlin, a data analyst at the Wildlife Trusts, who is autistic and dyslexic. Pete's current role involves improving the collection and use of data across the Wildlife Trusts and working on the commissioning of a new data facility. He's particularly passionate about the conservation sector being evidence-led; after all, we're in an ecological crisis and can't afford not to heed the evidence of our changing climate. He loves being able to influence cultural and systemic change from the ground up, and finds that most people in his field are quite like him, with lots of visual thinkers and people who thrive on detail, all working together to achieve a common goal.

To influence people, you must feel strongly enough about something in the first place and be able to connect that feeling to others. We could call this empathy, which in the context of neurodivergence is a fascinating topic. Typically, you'll read that diagnostically autistic people 'lack empathy', but this is yet another classic ableist observation. Autism is a 'social communication disorder', so surely this is more a question of not being able to communicate empathy, rather than not feeling it in the first place. It's just another example of a lack of knowledge, understanding and (cough) empathy, towards autistic people. How ironic. They may not always display empathy towards other people, but in my experience, they often demonstrate deep empathy towards 'things', such as animals, objects and situations that involve a clear-cut right and wrong. A 2022 study confirms this and outlines that difficulties with empathy in people with autism are specific to human relationships. Its authors hypothesize that because human beings are not as behaviourally transparent as various other types of animals, we're difficult for autistic people to decode emotionally. It's no surprise, then, that there's a growing body of research into the benefits of therapeutic interventions using animals, specifically for autistic people, alongside the vast evidence base for animal therapy in general.

In the early days of researching this book, I spoke to Eddie Brown, a student and wildlife education volunteer who is autistic. We discussed his deep empathy and connection with wildlife, which he described as 'an unavoidable awareness of the wildlife around him, whether it's a crustose lichen or a leaf-miner trail on roadside vegetation'. This awareness generates strong feelings of anger or sadness when nature is subject to mistreatment, and if he witnesses the destruction of any wildlife, he can't focus on anything else for days. Interestingly, this doesn't have to be the direct witnessing of environmental desecration; he can be affected, for example, by a news report about fox hunting. Eddie said that he hasn't yet found an effective way to externalise the emotions that arise in these scenarios, so they linger in his mind and body and can manifest as migraines, fatigue and depression. He's unable to look away or switch off, and suspects that if he wasn't autistic, he wouldn't experience emotional overload to this extent. I wondered if, with these negative impacts, this level of empathy for the natural world could potentially be harmful for Eddie's overall wellbeing?

He feels that at times, his hypersensitivity to nature can be detrimental and overwhelming, to the point where he can no longer use it as a positive attribute. However, at other times he can harness it, and this gives rise to situations where he feels that he is who he wants to be and wants to be who he is. He said that he could debate forever on whether his hypersensitivity is a good thing, but what it does do is increase his desire to connect with the natural world through learning about it. This, he said, is undoubtedly an asset, especially as it drives his internal obligation to reduce his environmental impact. He wonders if he wasn't so sensitive about nature, would he experience this as fully, or as deeply as he does? Would he be as sure of its importance? He doesn't think so. He believes that if he wasn't autistic, he might be able to look away from the damage we do. Take autism away, and that compassion towards wildlife and the environment has gone too. To me, that's not worth losing, at all.

Another facet of neurodivergence is the 'special interest'. The narrative around special interests traditionally aligns with autism, but more recently I've seen its use in conjunction with ADHD, and with neurodivergence in general. I don't particularly like the word 'special' in this context, and the National Autistic Society refer to this as having an 'intense interest'. These interests are a bit like a long-term version of hyperfocus, and as well as being intense and repetitive, they can sometimes become restrictive. Special interests, especially with autism, can start at a young age and may change, but are often lifelong. Some examples of these are things like emergency vehicles, dinosaurs, and specific television characters. Special interests are generally a positive thing. As well as being a source of wellbeing, they might also provide an autistic person with commonality and conversation starters to help navigate social situations. They can also offer comfort, stability, predictability and routine – words commonly associated with coping with neurodivergent conditions. With awareness and management, an intense interest can be advantageous to the wellbeing of an autistic person and even benefit them professionally. This seems to be the case for some of the people I've spoken to from the conservation sector.

Take Naomi, for example, who doesn't think that the term 'special interest' describes the all-encompassing nature of their fascination with wildlife, nor would they call it an obsession; rather, it's both their lifestyle and the lens through which they view the world. Whilst their interest is all-consuming – it's their job, their volunteering, their hobby, and their downtime – there isn't a stringent rule that everything they must do is wildlife-themed, it's just their preference. For example, Naomi also enjoys crafting, knitting and embroidery, but it will almost always be nature-themed because that's what they want to surround themselves with. They reflected that the only thing in life they'd also consider an interest, that has nothing to do with wildlife, would be eating ice cream. At work and when undertaking a wildlife survey, it never feels like a job to Naomi. They get to walk around and use all their senses, it's just that someone is paying them to write it all down and put it in a fancy report afterwards (their words, not mine). Naomi acknowledged that this could seem intense to an outsider, and it's exhausting for them, but they're certain their special interest makes them a better ecologist.

Larissa also recognises that her special interests in plants and invertebrates makes her more effective in her role. Botany is the clincher. Her ideal holiday is a botanical one, she's always reading and learning about plants, and she's always looking for connections and patterns, such as those in flowering times and plant associations. Along with her love for textiles through the use of a multi-shaft loom, she's now incorporating plant dyes into her work. She loves the alchemy of natural dyeing, as well as its roots in our cultural history. Whilst talking to her about this, I recalled an activity I once did at a forest school, bashing natural items between sheets of cloth, with a little hammer. It was awesome. This took me down a rabbit hole myself, which is somewhere that Dr Steve Allain the zoologist has been his entire life. A childhood obsession with dinosaurs became a lifelong special interest in amphibians and reptiles. He describes them as his 'everything'. In fact, he's comfortable calling it an obsession, but it's also his career. He does a lot of research, naturally, but also owns a vast collection of books, some dating back to the eighteenth century, a lot of art, and various niche collections, such as stamps.

The range of special interests in this sector is as you might expect. Gull enthusiasts. Earwig lovers. James Hankins, though, has a seriously niche obsession and wasn't afraid to tell me about it. Growing up on a Royal Farm estate, for him, it has always been about the farm machinery. He even set up a photo blog, Agricultural

Voyeurism, hiding in the bushes to take covert photos of heavy vehicles at work. I love this, especially that he didn't bat an eyelid as he told me about it. Some time after we met, I decided I wanted to dig a bit deeper and ask him what it is that he enjoys so much. It's everything. The sounds, the colours, the vibrations of big kit following its seasonal deployment, whether it's the clunking of big balers or the forage harvester chopping grass in spring. It's all about the sensory experience with James. He even sent me videos to try and express just what it is that grabs him about it. They didn't have the same impact for me, but isn't that the simplistic beauty of a special interest, anyway?

Master's student Şeniz Mustafa and I chatted a lot as I was writing this book. She had some brilliant insights and anecdotes to share. One of our conversations was about what attracts neurodivergent people to work in the conservation sector. Şeniz suggested that there may be a connection between people working in conservation and having a strong sense of justice. She also mentioned hyperfocus and deep empathy, and talked about how conserving the environment feels like the morally right thing to do. For some autistic people, rules, routines and morals can be very important, which can make them resistant to change but staunch advocates for integrity. Alister Harman is one of these people. He said his persistence, and willingness to stand his ground when he is sure of the facts, have enabled him to advocate for wildlife, even in the face of confrontation. He asked why anyone would challenge someone passionate enough about a subject to have retained all the information about it. Especially, he added, if the subject relates to law, which he describes as 'one of the most autistic-ideal rulebooks.'

This rigidity isn't a negative trait, and, as Alister was keen to point out, if you harness it, it's gold. In his experience, autistic people's sensitivity to problems should be seen as a positive opportunity to identify and remedy problems in the way organisations and groups function. I agreed with his sentiment and reflected on how the observations and ideas are often there, but the ability to socially communicate them is often the barrier. The Wildlife Trusts' Pete Tomlin certainly feels that neurodivergent people have a strong sense of justice, and thinks this is what probably attracts them to the voluntary sector in the first place. However, he sometimes wonders if the percentage of neurodivergent people employed in the voluntary sector is greater than that within the private sector. This was also suggested in a 2024 report I found that discussed 'neuroinclusion' in the workplace. A neuroinclusive workplace is one that 'consciously and actively includes all types of information processing, learning and communication styles.' The research found that employers in the voluntary sector are the most likely to say that their organisation values neurodiversity and are also most likely to state that they support neurodivergent individuals to perform at their best.

Another strength enjoyed by many neurodivergent people is the ability to confidently address people, even in large groups. Despite not being the biggest fan of people in general, I like to think I'm decent at working with them. It's exhausting to be a people person, when most of the time you'd prefer to be in your own company, but it can be a useful strength to have in your armoury. Şeniz says that she speaks a lot in her events-management role at university, and describes herself as a great talker, winning a little-miss-chatty award when she was at school. She doesn't mind this, as she talks with confidence, and has a great mantra: if you're going to talk a lot, talk well. Rather than this chattiness becoming a negative attribute, she feels it has grown into a strength she can utilise in many areas of her voluntary work. Public speaking, running workshops, making online videos; all these elements of her life benefit from her loquacity. It's the same for Tracey Churcher of the National Trust, who feels her biggest ADHD strengths are that she's warm, approachable and available for her team. She enjoys listening to their ideas, which she feels is enriching to her and her team.

I try my best to be constantly available for my own team, but it can be utterly exhausting. Spinning umpteen plates can be tricky, and I find that once you add in other people's tableware, you can easily drop one piece, several pieces, or all of it. Many people I spoke to felt they were adept at managing multiple projects at once, especially those with ADHD, but only a few of them went on to acknowledge the perpetual state of stress and anxiety this can leave you in. It can be a delicate balancing act to avoid what we know as burnout, which can cause symptoms akin to those of depression, and in neurodivergent people, can trigger shutdown, meltdown, and an increase in sensory sensitivity. Intensive masking, or forcing engagement in social interactions, can also be incredibly draining.

If you work in the conservation sector, why wouldn't you want to toil alongside those who demonstrate the types of skills and strengths described above? People who may have more empathy toward nature than their own species. People who approach seemingly impossible tasks from obtuse angles. People whose lives are acutely interwoven with the environment. People whose interest in the natural world runs deeper than you can possibly fathom; it's a part of who they are, an element of their very being. People who can focus so intensely on something that their outcomes and output surpass all expectations. People who experience the outdoors through an aura of sensory awareness. People who can locate patterns and trends in the most complex of places. People who inspire and lead, often through possessing a complete lack of filter, which allows people to see their vulnerabilities and grow to trust them implicitly. People who have a moral compass that only points in the direction of the natural world, fighting for what's right. Whether they think outside the metaphorical box, or approach a subject with pinpoint focus, or make connections where others don't, neurodivergent people absolutely do think differently to other people, and I know who I want in my corner.

It might be impossible to ever know the true numbers of neurodivergent employees in any sector. Either the data isn't available, or disclosures haven't been made, as there's still far too much stigma and ignorance when it comes to such diagnoses. On top of that, there will also be many neurodivergent people who have never sought a diagnosis or are yet to fully discover their differences. The conservation sector, as with many others, may employ large numbers of people with unique neurodivergent skillsets that never get drawn upon. I appreciate that the strengths in this chapter are just a snapshot of the attributes anyone can bring to any working role, whether neurodivergent or not. Perhaps neurodivergence amplifies these strengths. Perhaps it's the nature of the conservation sector itself that allows neurodivergent people the freedom to exhibit them. What I know for sure is that the stories and experiences described in these pages will reflect those of other neurodivergent people across the sector. As awareness grows, so will recognition, and hopefully this book can add to the narrative around neurodivergent strengths, and help other employment sectors become more neuroinclusive, to the benefit of neurodivergent people and their colleagues alike.

CHAPTER SEVEN

Cutting the toe pads off hundreds of dead parrots

Achievements

Exploring the conservation sector through speaking with a range of (mostly neurodivergent) professionals has been an enlightening experience. I began this research with a general lack of understanding about what the word conservation means, let alone the structure of the sector. This process of discovery has been so empowering that it bore a tangent of its own, driving me to investigate the incredible achievements of the people I've spoken to. A frustrating element of this has been that many people in conservation, despite recognising the wider environmental benefits of their work in terms of biodiversity, often don't see it as an achievement as much as a lifetime dedication. I see it as a foundation, where the achievements within all the jobs that make up the sector coalesce into the building blocks for future conservationists to continue piling on top. It's a never-ending vocation. Many of the people I spoke to ooze with an absolute affinity for the outdoors and wildlife. Their personal and professional lives often merge, ethereally, into an existence of dedicating life to other life. It's mutual, symbiotic and breathtakingly beautiful. They need nature as I believe I do.

One of the most fascinating people I spoke to was Thom Byrne. Thom has autism, and his experience at school was horrendous. He was almost on the receiving end of a permanent exclusion for lashing out when struggling, and his school just couldn't cope with his behaviour. Further and higher education were also tough, and although he had a support worker, he left with a lower grade than he was hoping for and minimal life skills. He feels lucky that he fell into various governmental jobs through the support of the Access to Work scheme, and found himself working across several high-profile departments, including the Department for Education and the Department of Health. Thom was instrumental during the Covid pandemic in helping to set up systems whereby people could test for the virus. Then, with slack in his team, and having to self-isolate, he put himself forward for redeployment. This was when he got a random phone call from the Department for Environment, Food and Rural Affairs (Defra) asking if he would like to be part of a team with a mandate for both 'financing green' and 'greening finance' on a global scale. An example of their work is helping to develop a 'global biodiversity credits roadmap' for supporting businesses to invest in nature recovery.

Thom openly told me that nature isn't his natural habitat; he can barely name any birds and spends most of his time on a computer. What he loves is working on big challenges and problems, so of course, he took the role. From there, he found himself working on a team crafting the text for the $12 billion Global Forest Finance Pledge at COP26, a global summit on climate change for countries who adhere to the United Nations Framework Convention on Climate Change (UNFCCC). He also wrote for both the G7 and G20 summits, where countries meet to discuss global economy, and on elements of the UK's international nature strategy. He says that one of the reasons he thinks he is so good at this, despite not having a background in nature, is his autistic wiring, which helps him get right into the detail of whatever he's working on. To help me understand the level of detail he went to, he told me how he built his own financial projection models, dug deep into historical data and read extensively on biodiversity finance.

He described how, with no preconceptions, he's able to zoom in on what's important, and shared an example of how far a special interest can go. In December 2022, the Convention on Biological Diversity was in negotiation, and in the months prior to this, all the top dogs were trying to figure out how much money they could realistically give to support developing countries to preserve, protect and restore nature, as part of what's called the Global Biodiversity Framework. What did they end up using? They used what Thom came up with after a few days of tinkering with logic models. Independent experts then came up with the same results. Thom strongly believes that the ingenuity, independence and forward thinking he used is where autistic people can really shine. He's immeasurably proud that his work made its way into a permanent international treaty and went towards securing actual money to support developing countries. With all these positive human impacts, we mustn't forget that he's made a huge and positive impact on the conservation of global wildlife, too. In a space overrun by master's degree holders, doctors and people with reams of climate and nature qualifications, the autistic brain came to the fore and made change happen.

Then, in 2023, some headhunting took place, and Thom was on his way to Dubai, to work on COP28. He went over there on a contract, not knowing anyone, but ready for the challenge. The host country, Dubai, had chosen mangrove restoration and protection as its own initiative to showcase alongside the formal negotiations about emissions that accompany the summit. Thom was given the task of creating large-scale events promoting mangrove restoration, with big flashy announcements and the projection of long-term impacts, basically out of nothing. It was stressful, 24-7 work, but he described it as amazing. It was his first time having complete autonomy over who his team should talk to, what they should be doing and what they were aiming for. The result was two huge events, with CEOs, government ministers and stars from National Geographic all sharing amazing stories about mangrove restoration and announcing to massive audiences that they had secured 49 governments (representing around 60% of the world's mangroves) as well as over 50 NGOs to endorse securing the future of 15m hectares of mangroves.

Thom is especially proud of elevating the voices of frontline community leaders, some of whom had left their countries for the first time, to speak at his event. He spent 11 months in Dubai before returning home.

He's now program managing the Natural Environment Investment Readiness Fund, which gives grants to environmental groups, local authorities, businesses and other organisations to help them develop nature projects in England to a point where they can attract private investment. The fund is overseeing around £50 million of government spending, and Thom describes it as part of the wider thinking around what England does to support funding of nature. I found his story incredible, and I love how his objective autistic brain has set him on a path to work at the highest levels of environmental policymaking and influence. This is a great example of where the specific strengths of a neurodivergent individual have been the catalyst for their environmental work, rather than their direct interest in it. It may be that having a less intense relationship with the environment allows Thom to take an objective view of his work, without the potential for a subjective influence from his feelings.

Many of the people I have spoken to have grown upwards, blooming into senior positions until arriving in the higher branches of the sector. This is exemplified by the story of Hazel Jackson of the Woodland Trust, whose incredible conservation experience has nothing to do with trees, and everything to do with parrots. Dead parrots. Hazel began her doctorate looking at the genetic makeup of ring-necked parakeets in the UK, to try and understand how they were thriving so well outside of their native range; but she soon found that collecting samples was going to be an absolute nightmare due to the logistics of catching enough parakeets to take DNA from. The UK's resident non-native parakeets would be easier to access, and in the end, she asked the public to send her shed feathers from parks and gardens. Collecting samples from throughout their native range (sub-Saharan Africa and southern Asia) would be an impossible task. Luckily, she heard about the Natural History Museum at Tring. She describes it as an amazing place, utterly surreal, with floor upon floor of historic bird specimens. These aren't all out on display; many are shut away in massive filing cabinets, which Hazel found out held at least 300 parakeets. So of course she had to go and visit, razor and specimen tubes in hand, to delicately cut tiny little bits of the toe pads from these birds, before taking them back to the lab to try and extract some DNA.

Some of these birds were from the late seventeenth century but were so well-preserved, she was able to safely get hundreds of little toe pads. It gets better. After cleaning out an old cleaning cupboard at her university, sterilising it and painting it, she set up her own mini lab; her 'ancient DNA lab'. The specimens were so delicate and susceptible to contamination that she spent many days alone, shut away, extracting DNA. While she was doing her PhD she heard about a potential project idea from the Seychelles Islands Foundation (SIF), which involved looking at the evolution of the black parrots that live there. At this point Hazel lit up, her enthusiasm both captivating and infectious. These birds are only on one island – Praslin – which Hazel said makes them a 'really special parrot'. Black parrots are also found across the Indian Ocean, for example in Madagascar, and the SIF was keen to know if their parrot was the same as the others, or a distinct species. She knew she had the skills to do it but couldn't leave her PhD.

The SIF found someone else, but it didn't quite work out. Hazel was desperate to take part and knew she was capable after all the museum specimen work, so she battled to be allowed to participate. This all took place in the middle of her doctorate, but she was able to take a sabbatical to join the research team. She was sent even more toepad samples to extract DNA from, and some contemporary samples from the Seychelles and various islands so she could look at their evolutionary distinctiveness. Hazel was keen to point out how unglamorous it all was, sat on her own in a university broom cupboard, arms in a fume hood, chopping up little bits of century-old parrot toe pads. However, after the project and her PhD were done, she was able to go to the Seychelles for a month and visit the Vallee de Mai nature reserve on Praslin. This natural palm forest contains the main food source of the Seychelles black parrot, the flowers of the coco de mer palm, which is also incredibly rare.

Hazel was able to see the parrots nesting. She even got to hold one, which she described as probably the most incredible moment of her life. She then had the opportunity to give a presentation to other conservationists, local people and the news in the Seychelles, and to lecture on her findings, which were that these black parrots, found on just one island in the Seychelles, were so evolutionarily distinctive that they were a unique species. This also gave a boost to the conservation of these birds, which Hazel is immeasurably proud of. She acknowledged how modest the fieldwork was but spoke of the deep joy in the unknowns of genetics, as you have no idea if any of your experiments are going to work until right at the very end when you get your results. The suspense of this, to Hazel, can be more engaging than being out in an exotic location, as the search for definition and clarity in experimentation really grabs her attention. It strikes me that this may well be a connection with the risk-taking tendencies of people with ADHD.

I love how Hazel's intensive study into parrot evolution, resulting in the discovery of a new species, shows the benefits of hyperfocus to answer a conundrum. I also love how solving the mystery of the ancestry of this black parrot will have a direct impact on its conservation. When I spoke to Hazel about it, or asked follow-up questions, she exuded enthusiasm for the project and her role in it. The sense of pride and wellbeing that must come from being part of a successful project like this must be immense.

Hazel wasn't the only person who shared a species-specific conservation success story with me; so too did Naomi Davis. Their experience was working on the Pine Marten Recovery Project (PMRP). The aim of this project was to translocate (not reintroduce) pine martens to mid-Wales, and it took place between 2015 and 2017. In this time, the PMRP brought 51 martens from Scotland to the release site and fitted them with radio-collars to track their movements. After this translocation period, the project went into a monitoring phase using scat (faeces) surveys and camera traps, to record animal movements and breeding. The whole project was, in Naomi's words, phenomenally successful, and evidence suggests that breeding has taken place every year since the translocation.

The project itself is undoubtedly fantastic, but what I find most powerful about Naomi's experience is the impact that it had on them. Back in 2015, they were in their third year of university, burnt out and suffering badly with chronic fatigue. To make matters worse, the accommodation they were in was dreadful, so not only did they feel like a prisoner in their own body, but also their own flat. Naomi was candid here, also sharing that they had very few friends, mostly from not having the energy to socialise due to the exhaustion of masking their autism. They had done some volunteering with the PMRP during the feasibility stages in 2014; a lot of walking round Welsh woodlands, which would be tiring enough for someone in full health, let alone someone with chronic fatigue. That said, Naomi leapt at the opportunity to help with the radio-tracking element of the project. It wasn't the most enthralling of job descriptions: spend eight hours in a truck driving around mid-Wales in the middle of the night, listening to white noise on a radio-tracker, all whilst managing the stress and expectations of the burnt-out colleague sitting next to you. But this outline read as pure perfection for Naomi, and it was. Like many neurodivergent people, they detest small talk, and even what they refer to as 'medium' talk. However, sitting for hours on end with nothing to do but converse means that 'big' talk is on the table from the start, which they were buzzing about. They built instant connections with their fellow volunteers. For the first time in an age, it felt OK to just be themselves. This meant that they could unmask and let their personality shine through, which is something that rarely happens for autistic people in the professional world. Naomi put every ounce of their energy into the project, which meant missing many lectures in their third year of university, but stands firm with this decision. The value of the project, both to their wellbeing and their career, outweighs the lower grade they eventually got in their degree. They played down their contribution, saying that they were just a source of conversation and a human audio stand, but they do acknowledge they felt like they had value, which was something previously missing from their life.

Over time, Naomi's health got better, and they were able to join the team on the ground to conduct scat surveys, which they usefully explained as 'walking around looking for pine marten poo'. Naomi's intense sensory perception made them an expert poo prospector, with a keen eye and the ability to remember the 'unique smell profile' (their words). This language is typical of the way that Naomi honestly and openly explained things to me – it was so refreshing. They went on to tell me that their enthusiasm for such tasks gave them the confidence and motivation to hone their dung detection (ok, my words there) skills and expand them to include all the tracks and signs that animals leave. They now lead walks and talks on these themes, all from the original platform of the PMRP. Their faeces ID skills are indisputable, and now whenever a picture of poo is put on the county wildlife social-media page, a tag to Naomi soon follows. They're known as the 'poo lady', although Naomi is keen to point out that they prefer 'poo wizard' for gender neutrality.

What the PMRP also gave Naomi were some fantastic opportunities to experience things behind the scenes, like being able to watch the martens move into their soft-release pens, and facilitating some filming sessions for the BBC's *Autumnwatch*. In the latter, it was known that the martens would usually go to the area outside a specific static caravan in a park site, where the resident would feed them. However, this person was away at the time of filming, and Naomi stood in as the official marten baiter.

What the project did for Naomi's career is powerful stuff. It gave them an opportunity to engage with conservation in a way that was accessible for them, somewhat ironically by offering work that would be inaccessible to most. Naomi was then offered some paid work during the closing stages of the project, radio tracking, camera trapping, and scat surveying – all the things they'd been doing already! All of this was welcome news at a time when Naomi had been struggling with both their physical and mental health. They had also felt like they were in a bit of a professional rut, stuck doing voluntary work, with nothing paid seeming to be available. Naomi describes the whole experience as life-changing.

From poo to pellets. Another role that many would consider unattractive is the research that Şeniz has been doing. In 2016, Knepp Estate, the UK's premier rewilding site, brought in some white storks. They had a rough idea of what their storks were eating, but there hadn't been any formal analysis. This is where Şeniz came in. In her third year of university, she knew that Knepp had a list of projects where they were looking for student help, but the projects were specifically for students studying for a master's degree. Nevertheless, in the spring, she contacted them about the white stork project and was accepted as a participant. She felt that since the storks were going to stay at Knepp, it could be interesting to have a look at how they interact with their environment and what that might look like once their population embeds and becomes viable. It made sense to look at Knepp's flying storks, rather than their flightless group, as the flying storks were able to leave the estate and roam the area. So the team's research was to study the extent to which the free-flying birds chose to forage for food on top of their supplementary feeding by the Knepp estate, the theory being that in order to maximise energy, if they don't have to forage, they won't.

How did they do this? By dissecting stork pellets, of course. Several times a day, white storks regurgitate all the bits of food they can't digest, in the form of a pellet. When Şeniz explained her research, she was always keen to point out that pellets are not faeces, so when they were scrabbling under nests to collect them, she says it may smell like a wet dog, but taking apart undigested prey is better than digested. The team found a variety of food items to quantify and weigh: mostly insects (beetles), worms, some snails, a vole and some non-edible items like stones and hair bands. There was a concern that the white storks might be eating endangered species, but they weren't found to be eating these species to the point where they would affect population size. Şeniz asked if I'd seen storks eat, which I hadn't, and her description made me chuckle. It's not a science, she said, more a case of, 'Does it move, yes it does, then it's food, and it can get in my massive beak!'

The hope is that the team's research will give some insight into whether the storks can solely rely on foraging, whenever Knepp decides to stop supplementary feeding. Şeniz sees this as a foundation for further studies, and hopes that she can be a part of them. It turns out that she has a special interest relating to pellet and foraging analysis. She has done pellet analysis on yellow-legged gulls for BirdLife Cyprus, research on the foraging and diet of common terns, and has led a barn owl pellet workshop too. As Şeniz says, 'If your hyperfocus leads you to do something niche, then do it, as it's unlikely anyone else will be.' Not only has the white stork project been beneficial for her career, but she has also worked alongside an incredibly supportive team of volunteers. She said that every moment in the lab was enjoyable, and every pellet was a learning experience, which may be gross and weird to some, but was magic for Şeniz. Oh, and as well as achieving professional satisfaction and conclusive research outcomes, she now has a load of beetle specimens at home. Beetles she found in pellets!

Alister Harman also had an incredible, and rather surreal, anecdote. He only gave it a passing mention when we first spoke, and I had to dig out some more information in a later conversation, as I thought it was well worth sharing, despite Alister's insistence that it was just a 'strange thing to happen'. In a previous role, Alister was given the task of caring for a tree that had been grown from a seed Tim Peake took to the International Space Station. What's even crazier is that the seeds came from the very apple tree at the home of Sir Isaac Newton that has long been thought responsible for dropping the apple that inspired the theory of gravity. The 'Pips in Space' project took several apple pips into space to float around in microgravity for six months, before coming back to Earth. After this they were planted and nurtured at Kew Gardens, where, although several seedlings didn't survive, a total of eight young trees resulted. Before these trees' dispersal around the country, organisations had the opportunity to bid for one, with them eventually ending up all over Europe.

Alister's role in all of this wasn't as glamorous as the concept, but in my mind, it is still awesome. The Catalyst Science Discovery Centre and Museum in Widnes won their bid to have one of the saplings, and as he was working for the local council at the time, Alister was given the responsibility of looking after it until some landscaping work had taken place. His role as the ranger overseeing the 'space sapling' was basically to water it and ensure it was kept healthy until planting. This then meant the end of his involvement, as the tree was planted in an area that he didn't manage. Even though I think the story of the space sapling is fascinating, the museum doesn't celebrate it much on their website, which I think is a shame. However, what I love about this story is how it brings together the domains of astronomy, physics, conservation and social history. Alister told me that he can still appreciate the journey of that seed, and that it makes you realise just how small our world is. It's redolent of the tree metaphors I wrote about earlier. Roots and branches. Growth and blossoming. It's yet another example of the networks underpinning all of this.

The next contribution came from a discussion with Inez Williams-King, who, alongside working as a senior landscape advisor within Natural England's Landscape, Heritage and Geodiversity team, runs the 'Grower' with her husband, Chris. The Grower is a bareroot tree and hedge nursery in Cornwall, growing several million broadleaf and conifer trees a year, for supply across the UK to everyone from local authorities to commercial tree nurseries. They're set up on Inez's fifth-generation, family-run farm, which has been organic for the last 20 years, but wasn't always arable. It was once a cattle farm, but in 2020 Inez's family made the tough decision to sell off their herd. Inez and Chris had the idea of starting a bareroot tree business on the farm, alongside the existing crops, after seeing a skills gap in commercial horticulture and forestry. They think they're the only large-scale grower of bareroot trees that embeds the tree production into the farm's five-year management rotation. They also practice regenerative agriculture, and don't use pesticides, peat or irrigation, in the hope of restoring natural processes over time.

The farm is so organic that Inez shared a brilliant little anecdote with me about it. In their second year of growing, they had a visit from an industry leader who on inspecting their beech tree crop, said, 'This beech is the cleanest [of pests] I've seen this year! What are you using?' When they said it was the ladybirds, he gave them a smile and said, 'No, really?'. In response to this, they were able to confidently explain how they're able to avoid using pesticides because of their investment in ecosystem services. Their aim is to grow their trees in a sustainable way that fits both their ethical and environmental responsibilities. Chris runs the practical side of the business, and Inez does the behind-the-scenes stuff, such as planning, engagement and outreach. She is dyslexic, and I wondered if her neurodivergence plays any part in any of this, and asked her if this was the case. She pondered and said that after spending so much of her life having difficulties with accessing information, she relishes in making the Grower as accessible and visible as possible.

She also mentioned that she employs 'outside the box' thinking, and that this helps with things like task allocation, problem solving and resource management. This is a fixture of the business conversations she and Chris have, as she's constantly questioning historic growing techniques and practices, and suggesting alternatives. Chris says that Inez's approaches give him fresh angles and ideas, and both feel that they draw strength from each other, pushing together towards more information-driven and proactive decisions. This harmonious collaboration wasn't instant though, and they had to work on their interactions to make them effective. For example, Inez needs to make notes and check things for clarity; if not, she can really struggle. It's also the first time that Chris has been working closely with someone who's neurodivergent, so there has been a lot of learning taking place. This is learning that they use in the management of their staff team, some of whom are also neurodivergent, and some of whom are new to the sector. As well as growing trees, since its inception in 2021, The Grower has been planting them as part of nature recovery projects and agroforestry (the integration of trees into agricultural systems). This amounts to approximately 65,000 trees across Cornwall, and 5,600 trees across their farm. It's hard to put into words just what an incredible and inspirational thing this is.

This is just one statistical achievement that Inez detailed for me in a concise printed list that also featured awards, certifications and accreditations. What's most humbling about Inez is that The Grower isn't about her, or these awards, and what she wanted to celebrate the most was The Grower's staff and how by investing in their team, they have invested in a resilient business for the future. This is what she's deeply proud of, to be able to create positive change, not only in the landscape around us but also in the workplace. Whether we like to admit it or not, our society discriminates against people who are different. Its routines and structures, the frameworks that theoretically should work for those of us with haphazard neurons, aren't made with us in mind. To put it bluntly, our starting point is behind that of everyone else anyway. It can be tough enough when you're neurodivergent, but imagine adding in some other protected characteristics for good measure. What if you stand under a range of metaphorical umbrellas? Is there a greater impact on you embarking on a conservation career?

There's an enduring narrative in all these stories, and it's one we lose sight of as we immerse ourselves in the details: everyone sharing their experience here is neurodivergent. They have been given a diagnosis because they perceive and respond to the world around them in different ways to those who are deemed to be neurotypical. I'm not saying that their neurodivergence is the reason they've done these wonderful things, but what I want you to consider is this. To get to the point in their lives and careers whereby these opportunities have arisen won't have been easy at all. Many will have had these golden moments fall into their laps. Most, though, will have had to overcome often multiple barriers. Whatever the origin of these obstacles, the chances are that at some point, they rose from some form of discrimination. It's about time that we had a look at the landscape of the conservation sector through a different lens.

CHAPTER EIGHT

Are you here to make the tea or take the notes?

Barriers to access

Peering across from the education sector, the conservation sector seems a bit intimidating. As you might expect, many educationalists have high levels of education themselves, but the conservation sector is something else. It is literally brimming with designations. Floods of letters jostle after names: doctors, professors, and lists of acronyms that can cause a dyslexic person to panic. Various people that I know have told me conservation is a difficult profession to enter, as have most of the people I've spoken to for this book. It seems this is largely due to a preference for graduates to have undertaken considerable hours of voluntary work while holding higher-level formal qualifications in their spheres. I get the logic, as it's a practical vocation, but the requirement to undertake voluntary work must be such a barrier to anyone with any prior commitments: time, expenditures, children, work or geographical location. There's also a consensus on how painfully competitive the sector can be; often seeming nearly impossible for a lot of people to enter. For someone writing a book that champions inclusion, this institutional exclusivity is frustrating, to say the least.

My research began with the work of Brian Heppenstall, who has been working in the conservation sector for 27 years, from practical ecology roles to his current post teaching wildlife, ecology and conservation at a college in the south-west of England. I got in touch with him, and he was happy to share his views with me. Brian got into the sector through 'hard work, some luck – but almost no help or encouragement from anyone.' The lack of support across much of the sector motivates him to provide it for those in the early stages of their conservation careers, which I think must make him an awesome teacher. As we spoke about the expectations of many organisations in the sector, he described how he struggles with recruitment practices and the level of competition for the majority of jobs. What about the requisite for applicants to have a truckload of voluntary experience for most roles? This bothers Brian, as it creates an imbalance by offering better opportunities to those who can afford to work for free. As an outsider, I do wonder if the sector is intrinsically excluding anyone who isn't in a position of financial privilege to start with.

In 2019 Brian wrote an excellent article for the Countryside Jobs Service, exploring whether conservation is an accessible industry. As well as the need for experience and qualifications, one of the things that he found upon asking 40 of his former students about their route into the sector was that recruitment processes were off-putting. Some of his key observations were that employers provide little or no feedback to applicants (although this happens in all sectors), job descriptions were often confusing, and some people felt there was bias at the interview stage. Brian and I spoke about this, and he was clear that he has recently seen changes in the sector, with some employers taking a more holistic approach to recruitment. What does he mean by this? He has heard of a few organisations that now look for specific traits and characteristics in prospective candidates, rather than just knowledge and experience. He uses the National Park authorities as a specific example, some of which no longer use wildlife identification tests as part of their selection process, and now look for personality traits, like enthusiasm. As Brian points out, you can have all the knowledge and voluntary experience, but it still doesn't necessarily make you the right person.

It's easy for me to pass opinions on recruitment in the conservation sector, but having no actual experience of this myself, I knew I'd have to speak to a range of people and unpick what it's like to try and secure employment in it. I gathered anecdotes from a range of individuals, and not just those who identify as neurodivergent, as barriers and discrimination affect everyone. It took a while to drum up interest and contributions, but eventually I began to receive a variety of responses. They didn't always make pleasant reading, though. For example, one respondent, a young woman, even after obtaining a zoology degree found it 'impossible' to get a job in the sector despite her high grades. What was most frustrating was that she would apply for an entry-level role and hear that it went to someone who already had decades of experience. She occasionally got some feedback when unsuccessful, and recalls one such entry-level job that involved bird identification with an environmental agency. The successful candidate had simply been able to identify a greater number of uncommon birds. It makes sense, given the role, but stretches the meaning of 'entry-level' yet again, and echoes Brian's perspective too.

I came across an interesting blog by Georgina Mayhew, who's an environmentalist, writer and aspiring changemaker in her early thirties. After her own experience in the sector, she felt an obligation to share it and shatter some of the illusions about this line of work. She described her experience as, 'Years of degrees, rejection, debt and unpaid volunteering' before landing what she thought would be her dream job in conservation; a job where she was playing her part in shaping landscape restoration projects across Europe. However, after four years, she left the role, with a different perception of the sector. She described how she had dreamt of a fantasy version of conservation that was never there. The rose-tinted glasses she went in wearing came out with a spattering of alpaca faeces, the result of one of many unpaid voluntary roles. She spoke to many people, unearthing similar stories to the ones I have discovered, but from the inside she encountered colleagues and peers who work long into the night to meet unrealistic deadlines and have even had to apply for grants to fund their own jobs.

She noted the constant empty promises to create a more diverse workforce, then the next day seeing the same organisation advertise a full-time post with a salary of £18,000 a year. You can't gloss over the exploitation that so evidently occurs in this sector. So Georgina stuck her head above the parapet in what some people may consider career suicide, but she felt that if no one spoke up, these issues and barriers would continue to be swept under the carpet. However, as Georgina writes, right now, more than ever, we need people to unite and fight for our environment. Despite everything, she's still optimistic about finding a way to contribute to the causes she cares about without burning herself out. She says that it has taken her a long time to realise that jobs, cultures, social norms and expectations are all just fiction.

I considered that if I only reached out to people who've had difficult experiences, I was probably only going to receive anecdotes with an undercurrent of bias and bitterness; but what if everyone who has ever made it upwards in the conservation sector comes from a position of privilege? I wondered if class and socio-economics played a role in this, so I decided to speak to someone who I'd seen speak out on social media about socio-economic barriers in the sector, Mya Bambrick. Mya is a 20-year-old ecology and conservation student, whose interest in the natural world began when she was 8, in stark contrast with her hobby at the time: street dance. Her grandparents were passionate about the outdoors, but none of her other family members were, so Mya's own focus on wildlife came from watching the television programme *Springwatch*. Growing up in urban Crawley, her blossoming interest made her somewhat of an outsider with her peers. She rarely saw other young people at nature reserves, and those she met certainly didn't share her background. In fact, Mya and I have had similar childhood experiences, both coming from working-class, single-parent households. The struggle is, in our stories, very real.

For example, although Mya had a desire to meet people her own age who also had an interest in nature, with no access to a car, and unable to pay for expensive public transport, she could only do this through social media and wildlife forums. Later, when she began pursuing a career in the conservation sector, she found out that she would have to undertake a range of practical experiences. However, Mya feels that because of her socio-economic background, she was unable to access these experiences as easily as others might. Of course, she understands that many charitable organisations run on minimal budgets, but renumerating young people, rather than relying on wealthy volunteers, would potentially increase access to this sector. She says that there is a systemic problem when it comes to paying young people for things like writing articles and giving talks. We both agreed that the expectation on people to work for free, just for experience and exposure, is utterly wrong. We have both been in this situation, which is not only personally devaluing, but can be made worse when people from positions of privilege receive fees for similar work.

Mya discussed other barriers to people from diverse socio-economic backgrounds entering the conservation sector and connecting with nature, including access to transport, lack of facilities at reserves and personal safety concerns when visiting reserves on her own. Back when she kept lists of birds, her inability to cadge lifts and travel long distances was often disheartening; especially when she heard other people discussing the rare birds they'd seen. She made a salient point that being respectful of other people's situations is vital.

The social isolation Mya experienced was transformed when she discovered the existence of organisations offering opportunities that she could access, despite her background. The British Trust for Ornithology, for example, runs a fabulous youth engagement programme, for which Mya is now a youth representative. Through funding from the Cameron Bespolka Trust, a charity set up in memory of its namesake with the aim of connecting young people with nature, she went to a bird camp in 2016, which she described as life changing. She met other young people and went to nature reserves that were otherwise unreachable; opportunities that she wouldn't have had if it wasn't for the Trust's financial support. Genuine possibilities for hard-to-reach people come from vital work like this, and we should be celebrating them as much as we can.

What is it like to enter the sector from a position of privilege? I spoke to a 30-year-old Scottish man, who felt that a combination of factors was at play when cementing his own career in conservation. Towards the end of university, he realised he needed to gain more experience, and he reflected on just how lucky he was to be in a secure-enough financial position to be able to volunteer. He also made it onto a young birders training course, which gave him the opportunity to gain personal and professional contacts, one of which led to some short-term work. However, he candidly acknowledges that throughout all of this, he got financial support from his parents between roles; a luxury that many other wannabe conservationists don't have. A year of volunteering at Edinburgh Zoo was his gateway into the sector, and eventually he landed a paid role as an assistant zookeeper. Alongside higher education, the contacts he made through his various opportunities were the main catalysts for his career development, but we must remember that these all came from a position of privilege.

The barriers that disadvantaged young people face when trying to enter the conservation sector also extend into formal recruitment processes. Each year, the organisation Racial Action for the Climate Emergency (RACE) releases an annual report on diversity in the environmental sector. In their 2024 review, 67 of the 142 contributing organisations (47 per cent) purport to be adjusting their recruitment processes to reflect that having a degree and extensive work experience is no longer an essential criterion for a role. A strong claim, which clashed with some of what I was hearing, so I began to delve into the mechanisms of various organisations in the sector. I began starting discussions with people on the ground to try and get some insight into their recruitment experiences. One response was particularly powerful: that of Andrew Whitelee, who had been working in IT for 12 years and then, as part of what he believes was an early midlife crisis, chose to pursue his passion for wildlife by returning to university to study for an ecology degree. He had some money behind him, unlike many of the younger members of his cohort, some of whom quit.

At the end of his studies, it quickly became clear that graduate pay in the conservation sector is not in any way commensurate with the cost of completing a degree in the first place. In fact, as entry salaries were so low, Andrew took on some lecturing at the university he had just left, as the pay was so much better. It also meant he could add to his transferable skills for when he felt ready to tackle the higher echelons of the conservation sector pyramid. In his position of experience and authority, he felt he had a duty to prepare his own students for the reality of what was coming, and he constantly told them to try and volunteer whilst they were studying. The reality was that many of his students had to work unsociable hours in the retail and hospitality sectors to fund their education. Andrew also reflected on the advertising of long-term voluntary roles by the RSPB and the National Trust, describing it as 'deeply frustrating'. Yes, these were often wonderful opportunities to learn and practise in beautiful settings, but these can be unrealistic for people without financial backing, and often did not lead to a paid role anyway.

Although long-term volunteering in the conservation sector doesn't necessarily result in paid work, this is nevertheless often the goal for those undertaking it. Many could be taken for a bit of a ride; driven by a sector that seems to have made voluntary experience necessary for most practical roles. It feels like a manipulation of an unpaid labour force – a huge force when you consider some of the volunteer numbers at the largest organisations, such as the National Trust. Andrew pointed out that when he was scouring the graduate job market back in

2007, the pay was £12,000 a year at best. It simply wasn't sustainable for younger people unless they had significant financial support. In this way, the sector is at risk of creating what might come across as an exclusive demographic. Considering the findings of the RACE report, where organisations claimed to be making their recruitment processes more equitable, I wondered how much of it is lip-service.

Then I spoke to Ajay Tegala, a ranger and wildlife communicator, about how he got into a sector he described as 'competitive', which he thought was due to an almost glorious perception of it to outsiders. I certainly understood what he was saying; it seems like the dream career when you see it on social media. He was clear that it is, of course, a rewarding and enjoyable vocation, but he's also a realist and said that the route in, as well as the job itself, is often difficult and requires physical and mental dedication. Ajay said that in his experience, most, if not all his colleagues have undertaken conservation volunteering for at least a year, including some he's met who have been working for over 20 years. Not only does this support the notion of an *absolute* requirement to have undertaken significant amounts of voluntary work, but it also shows that recruitment practices can be biased. I respect the fact that he's open enough to admit how lucky he is to have been able to volunteer when he was younger and still studying, but that if he had to do it all again now, without any support, he would find it incredibly daunting and financially challenging.

Many aspects of the conservation sector come with a financial cost. The best equipment can cost thousands of pounds, and there are also costs associated with clothing and travel. It's an expensive business. Şeniz, like Mya, reflected on the cost of travelling to conservation events, especially when you don't drive. Getting to the site might take several trains, buses or taxis. The cost of learning to drive can be prohibitive to anyone from a position of deprivation or poverty. I know that I didn't get my licence until I was in my mid-twenties, as it wasn't even an option for me before then. Today it is thought that to be successful in the conservation sphere, you must have a significant social media presence, and it may well be that some of its more prominent younger voices are monetizing their online engagement to fund their conservation careers.

Privilege may come from our socio-economics and demographics, but it encompasses many things, including our ethnic backgrounds. Back to Ajay, who is Asian British, and who has observed that since he began working in the conservation sector in 2012, ethnic diversity has barely risen at all. The RACE report concurs with him, literally opening with the line, 'The environment, climate, sustainability and conservation sector is one of the least racially diverse in the country.' A pitiful 6 per cent of staff across 142 organisations identify as people of colour. Only 39 of the organisations report on equality, diversity, and inclusion (EDI) annually, yet 61 claim that they regularly review the effectiveness and impact of their EDI activities. Eighty-eight organisations give a senior leader responsibility for EDI, yet it's striking how little is genuinely being put in place by way of strategic action in this area. What I gleaned from the RACE report is that there are many initiatives and strategies, but not much action. It's basically EDI lip-service. This came up repeatedly in my research and interviews, vehemently so when I spoke to Aisha Mahmood, who is Pakistani, and works for the Birmingham & Black Country Wildlife Trust.

Firstly, she mused that the 'right to decide how we protect the environment has historically (and in her opinion, currently) sat with the elite in the UK, which means that the sector has various mechanisms in place to gatekeep who can work in it' – we know that this places emphasis on qualifications and experience, usually gained on a voluntary basis. She added that most people of colour over 16 are from immigrant families, where there's an expectation to get 'proper' jobs and achieve the better lives their families came here for in the first place. Mix all this up and a huge chasm appears between people of colour with a flourishing interest in conservation, and the opportunities their prospective employers believe they should have had access to. The reality of becoming a naturalist or conservationist could be far away for someone from an immigrant background, all just to protect and preserve our planet, and not get paid very much. If you get your foot in the door, Aisha noted, you're often one of the only people of colour and can often be made to feel like an outsider, whether this is intentional or not.

What she thinks is a bigger issue now is that the sector still has quite a paternalistic approach that it can't seem to shake. What does she mean by this? It's the idea that diversity is a 'thing we must do', where we just upskill more people of colour or employ young people of colour to then mould into the same image of conservation that was excluding them in the first place. What Aisha outlined to me were the archaic beliefs that there's only one way to protect the land, and only white people know how to do it. She feels that this culture spreads into most new EDI strategies. Why not listen to the experiences of people from diverse ethnic backgrounds, their own heritages, their intergenerational protection of the environment, and their cultural habits often rooted in the reverence of nature? She ended by stating that when diversity is seen as having people of colour within a failing structure, versus the process of diversifying solutions and rebuilding what isn't working, then everyone is being let down.

Another point that Ajay was keen to make is how he feels that the gender imbalance in the sector has seen improvements but is by no means even. When I spoke to Binnies flood and coastal consultant Emily Clarke, her immediate response was that the main barriers facing her had been her gender and her age. She has been asked if she's 'there to make the tea or take the notes?' She also recalled a few other anecdotes, one when she was a senior flood risk officer at Cambridgeshire County Council and was on a site visit to a farm. The farmer wouldn't talk to her, only her male colleague, who she was teaching. Her colleague kept 'deferring to the expert' (Emily), but the farmer kept directing questions to him and not Emily. Or another time at an event when she went to put her coat up in a self-serve cloakroom, turning around to find three men were waiting to give her their coats. She couldn't help but just point to the sign saying 'self-service', leaving them all red in the face.

She reflected that the sector can often feel predominantly male but is slowly evolving. More people of other genders are coming into the sector at the lowest level, and over time, they filter upwards. She has seen some questionable appointments though, where people who aren't necessarily good enough for a job are given it, just to satisfy some sort of diversity quota. Emily was adamant that she'd never want to be given a job because of her gender or age, only because she's the right person to do it. She's so passionate about this that she leads a committee for women who work in flooding and coastal erosion risk management, providing networking opportunities to help women in the sector share their experiences and feel more confident about applying for senior roles. She also introduced me to someone who works on EDI in the environment sector. Her name is Lea Nightingale, and she works for the Chartered Institute of Ecology and Environmental Management, otherwise known as CIEEM. For three days a week she works as an environmental analyst, and for the other two she works as the CIEEM's EDI engagement officer; an area in which they're doing some incredible work.

She said that the two issues of inclusivity and access to the sector that resonated with her the most are the reliance on unpaid volunteering and the need for a degree for most entry-level positions. This correlated with the general feeling I'd been getting. The CIEEM is working to remove these barriers by collaborating with organisations to dig deeper into what they're really looking for when they state 'volunteering' and 'degree' as criteria for a role. It has done this in partnership with Lantra, one of the UK and Ireland's leading awarding bodies for training in land industries. This led to a report on vocational pathways into the sector, with the overarching advice that work in conservation would be more attractive to young people and mid-career changers if vocational 'soft skills' were as desirable to employers as academia seems to be. As well as this, the CIEEM has also been working with the Wildlife and Countryside Link (a group of 86 environmental and wildlife organisations) on the creation of a 'route map to greater ethnic diversity' and with Lexxic (a neurodiversity inclusion organisation) on its internal processes and wider education around neuro-inclusion. It feels like Lea is part of a new wave of people in the conservation sector who are striving to make it more inclusive and diverse.

Who else is breaking down barriers with their work? The Conservation Equity Project (CEP), one of the founders of which is Alice Armstrong, is a new non-profit community-interest company formed with the aim of increasing diversity in the conservation sector. Alice did this alongside Tyler Williams-Green (the chief executive of the Out Runners, an inclusive running organisation) and Patrick Campbell (senior reptile curator at the Natural History Museum). The CEP offers mentorship and paid internships at leading conservation institutions to the next generation of budding Black British conservationists. The situation is bleak, as we've seen from the RACE report, and providing paid opportunities to early career Black British conservationists has never been more imperative. Alice also shared some research with me showing that people of colour are far less likely to volunteer for a club or group that helps the environment. What this means is that people of colour are effectively losing out on invaluable opportunities, networks and career prospects because of the recurring and underlying theme of having to volunteer. Offering paid experiences explicitly for Black people is just one of the many ways we can seek to address this issue, something they're doing at the CEP.

Another fantastic example is the work of Karen Ritchie, who is the chief executive of the organisation Bright Green Business. Amongst various environmental functions, it runs a student/graduate placement programme to help people gain the vital practical experience they don't necessarily know they'll need, to function in the sector. Karen feels strongly that everyone deserves to be paid for their work, so these placements are all paid at the Living Wage rate. Why did she start this initiative? Well, 20 years ago after achieving a degree in ecology, Karen couldn't find a job that didn't require a lot of experience, even when offering to work for free just to get a foot in the door. Even two decades ago, the same barriers to working in the conservation sector were in existence. It seems things have been stuck like this for a long while. It's refreshing to see so many people and organisations taking action to reduce and remove these barriers, but only time will tell us whether their hard work has been successful. I still think that the biggest issues affecting access to jobs in the conservation sector are knowledge and wealth, both being a byproduct of privilege.

Providing meaningful conservation careers information can be an absolute game-changer, but I have yet to see anything in any of the schools I've been working in over the last decade. A colleague of mine, who leads on careers, said that no organisations have ever come forward to offer any information sharing or outreach, and if he was to arrange something, it would have to be done by him. Yet renewable energy and sustainability are constant themes in the careers speaking calendar. Şeniz echoed this, saying that she had no conservation careers advice at school, sixth form, or university, not even a meaningful presence at a careers fair. She has always had to take the initiative and find things out for herself. But what if you're just not capable of doing that? I paused and reflected on the minute number of young people in my teaching career who've had a deep interest in the outdoors and in pursuing careers within it. One springs to mind, who I'd say is an environmental activist, but in a very microcosmic way, as they also had significant difficulties with social communication. If we hadn't sat with him to explore work experience placements, or to consider vocational pathways after school, I'm not sure he'd have done either.

Many of us would reference an inspirational teacher or family member as the person who lit the nature spark for us. Unfortunately, for many young people, this is one of the largest and most obvious barriers to accessible nature connection; they just don't have these people in their lives. As generations shift, the disconnect grows wider. Equitable access to green spaces is all well and good, but we need people who can enthuse and educate in a language that everyone can understand. All the people I've spoken to have overcome various barriers to work in this sector and it's their (often negative) experiences that add weight to the wider narrative here. Whilst it's awful that they've had to go through this, it helps shape the future for others, and I thank them for sharing with me. So, what can we do to help people, especially those who are neurodivergent, once they are working in the conservation sector? It's time to talk about reasonable adjustments.

CHAPTER NINE

Why is there a lump of multi-coloured playdough on my seat?

Reasonable adjustments

You may have heard of the term 'reasonable adjustments', and if you have then you likely have a rough idea what it means. You may think it's just business jargon, but these protections are laid out in law. Originally appearing in the Disability Discrimination Act, which then became the Equality Act, the concept has been around since the 1990s. The equality act imposes a duty on all employers to make reasonable adjustments to provisions, criterions, practices and/or physical features, to ensure that all employees, particularly those with a disability, can access their jobs on a level playing field. This can also mean the implementation of an internal/auxiliary aid to help with this. Failure to comply, quite simply, is discrimination. I should be clear that the word 'reasonable' is incredibly important here. An employer does not have to change the fundamental aspects of a job but must seek to reduce or remove any disadvantage that arises from a disability or protected characteristic. However, this must also be practical, affordable and safe for the employer and other employees. Of course, there will be variations of what multiple people deem to be 'reasonable'.

Ultimately, you must take responsibility and choose whether to tell your employer about your disability, health problem or condition. If your employer doesn't know, they can't make any adjustments, and you have no protections. It's that simple. You can usually disclose this in an application form, in a tick box, with no specific details – supposedly to protect you from discrimination. You can also share this information in an interview, and there is a question steering towards this in most of them. I choose to declare my own diagnosis at the application stage, but it's a personal choice and you don't even have to declare anything if having a disability isn't what you recognise or identify with. From the other side, receiving an application declaring a disability can result in a range of reactions from recruiters. Some might think it makes them appear more reputable if they employ people with disabilities. I know this happens, and I think it's a shocking attitude. But attitudes can play a big part in recruitment decisions, and sometimes the mere mention of a disability leads to assumptions that someone won't be able to do a job because of this.

The disability tick box can strike fear into any employer. Fear that they could be put under pressure to implement all manner of snazzy adjustments and adaptations if they so much as consider recruiting a particular candidate. However, these changes can be minor, requiring little to no effort to implement. They can be put in at the very beginning of an employment, even as early as the application process itself. A fantastic example of this is one I've seen recently on social media, where prospective applicants were able to read their entire application as a video and submit it that way. What a fantastic way to help navigate anxiety or social communication issues, for example. There are many articles about inclusive interview practices, and the majority suggest this approach to be one of the easiest to utilise. There are also lots of references to strengths- and skills-based interviews, where questions or tasks explore a candidate's capabilities and personalities objectively, rather than relying on their self-assessment. This, and the standardisation of interview questions, can help to remove what is known as unconscious bias, where an interviewer's preconceptions (usually misconceptions) about a certain group of people can cloud their judgement. Again, this is another form of discrimination that people who are neurodivergent experience in their professional lives.

Although I work in the education sector, not the environmental one, career choice is irrelevant when it comes to reasonable adjustments. I have generally been quite lucky with my workplaces in this regard. At the school where I began the diagnostic pathway, I felt I couldn't really ask for much to support me without the formality of a diagnosis. They were decent though, and let me have a small quiet office to myself and sent me all my working tasks in writing. Looking back, I can see now that these two accommodations were just as much for their benefit as they were for mine. I was kept out of the way and on top of my workload, which is a good example of how adaptations can be mutually beneficial. The time at my next school wasn't such a positive experience. They did buy me some excellent noise-cancelling headphones, but that was about it. I could have been given much more support, especially as I was new to middle leadership in schools; and in the end, stepping aside and then moving on became the only option. It was a steep learning curve for me, and still shapes my practice now, but as far as adjustments go, my next job couldn't have been any more different.

My formal diagnosis came at the same time as I took a temporary role on a permanent basis. This meant that I was able to declare having ADHD at my interview and then on the employment paperwork upon receiving a job offer. The human resources team immediately sent me a template for a 'workplace disability passport'. This fantastic formal document serves as a guide to what works for me and what can be put in place to support me. There's nothing groundbreaking on it, or anything that comes with a financial cost. Just simple things, like giving me all tasks and instructions in writing, giving me deadlines a week early, not giving me cryptic messages, and if you see me strutting around the school – it's a legitimate movement break. These things protect me, reduce anxiety in the workplace, but also make me more productive and efficient. It's refreshing to see these things in writing and highly empowering to know that a document exists that sets out how other people should work with you. The shoe is finally on the proverbial other foot. Rather than having to mould into what an employer and colleagues think you should be, they're the ones that have to adapt.

Unfortunately, employers don't always make adjustments, as one of the contributors found out, not once, but twice. The contributor was keen to remain anonymous and will, but for context only, I'll share that they are dyslexic. We spoke online one evening and immediately hit it off. Their first negative experience was a struggle from the start; with awful management, no training and a lack of support. This person decided not to name the employer, but confirmed that it was within the conservation and wildlife sector. They disclosed their dyslexia, informing the employer at the application stage. However, when following up on some issues this person had experienced with their manager, who they felt was being particularly difficult and unsupportive, the human resources team were adamant they hadn't made a disclosure at any point. Thankfully, this person had kept a record of every piece of paperwork and was able to prove that they had, indeed, provided this information. This didn't stop an extension of their probation period due to their manager being off work for a while following an accident, which understandably made them feel paranoid.

This was when they began to struggle in the role. Mainly through feelings of isolation, and not having a connection with anyone. I did find it sadly amusing when the person said it was basically them, a bunch of sheep, occasionally some volunteers, a farmer and a lot of wildlife. There were no public visitors, as the site wasn't open yet. I couldn't help but think that this sounds like the blissful environment that so many of the autistic naturalists I've spoken to yearn to work in. Things got worse when this person's boss, who I was starting to think was struggling themselves, began to send what they described as 'weird' emails, and calling them at eight o'clock in the evening to talk for hours. They began to feel caught up in a situation they couldn't escape from. They then felt it was the right time to start looking for other roles, and it was, as shortly after this the human resources department sent an invitation for a formal meeting. Pre-empting what this meeting might entail, this person found another role so that when they met, they got in first by resigning.

But they didn't back down. By fighting for equity and inclusion, they're fighting for what is right and just for everyone. After leaving, they wrote to the organisation's chief executive, outlining their experience and how they felt more should have been done about the questionable practices and attitude of their now ex line manager. They got what they say was a diplomatic reply, an acknowledgement containing nothing more substantial than a generic apology. They thought about taking the organisation to an employment tribunal but didn't feel confident enough in the process and protections. We went deeper. They described how they told their old line manager what they might struggle with or how they could benefit from some additional support. The line manager's response was to shut them down and ask why they 'just can't learn stuff?' By 'stuff', the line manager meant learning all the sections of their site, the names of all the fields, and all the specific species. 'Stuff' that this person had been clear they would need extra time to process. If only they had just been allowed to use their map as a prompt when speaking to contractors, the problem wouldn't have arisen, but the line manager wouldn't even allow them this small concession.

We talked about their current role at an organisation that takes reasonable adjustments far more seriously. A conversation about what could help them access their role effectively took place at the beginning of their employment, they were given computer software to support with office tasks and a tablet to take out on site. They also praised the induction and occupational health processes, which meant, basically, that everything was ready for them to hit the ground running. What has also been insightful for them is that they now line manage a small but largely neurodivergent team, and find themselves in a fantastic position to work with the new organisation on identifying and sourcing these people's reasonable adjustments, too. But it hasn't always been easy. For example, one staff member requires a lot of written information, but they're not necessarily the best person to create that. Therefore, they work collaboratively to explore ways they can meet each other's needs. I love this, and I love the fact that they're open with their team about their dyslexia. They even use an email signature saying that if the recipient didn't understand anything in the email, to please get in contact with them to clarify it.

Lucy Morris, who also had a horrific experience in education, is another superb example of the positive impact that reasonable adjustments can have, after not having them for so long. When a college finally gave her the opportunity to study with them, she got herself a place on a level-three wildlife and conservation course. She described the fact that she even got an offer as a complete shock, after facing so many barriers and rejections. She and her mum say that the college took one look at her EHCP, and rather than say they couldn't meet her needs, they went straight into how they were going to make it work. It almost felt unreal after everything she'd been through. The college put so many different adjustments in place for Lucy, including seating at the front of the class, giving her presentations in advance and including subtitles on them, and providing her with access arrangements for examinations. She described her lecturers as amazing, and said that she felt they had the knowledge and acceptance to work with her. Lucy got three distinctions at her graduation last year. A testament to her resilience and the college's dedication to supporting her.

One of the most obvious and prevalent adjustments is what we now call 'flexible working' or 'hybrid working'. I don't recall this being a common approach to work before the Covid pandemic, where many of us had no choice but to work from home. There were, of course, both positives and negatives to this, but for those of us who are neurodivergent and may struggle with the restrictions of being in an office or needing to mask all day just to fit in with a team, the idea of being able to escape was bliss. In April 2024, a government bill came into law whereby an employee has the right to request flexible working from day one of employment, rather than after 26 weeks. In the face of a rejection, an employee must be given a clear reason why, and has the right to appeal. Other changes include the right to make two requests for flexible working in a twelve-month period, rather than one, and the decision must now be made in two months, rather than three.

In a more general sense, flexibility is also being able to work part-time, and in job-sharing agreements, which can be hugely beneficial to neurodivergent employees too, especially those who tend to burn out. It can also refer to the changing of start and finish times. This may be to accommodate other commitments, such as childcare, or to arrive before or after colleagues and mitigate any sensory or social sensitivities.

Managing a team that works in various locations and at various times brings its own challenges, so there are positives and negatives with this. Having clear and agreed channels of communication is imperative, as is agreeing their frequency, as some neurodivergent people may need more, or less, interaction than others. On this note, adhering to communication preferences is another common and easy-to-implement adjustment, and something that almost all the contributors to this book mentioned when we discussed their own adjustments. This may be by communicating clear expectations and deadlines, or by committing tasks to lists and calendars, to aid organisation. It may be an acceptance of less-formal emails, to mitigate any difficulties with written communication. Some people prefer to use messaging platforms, or make a phone call, or have an online meeting. Some people require frequent praise and affirmation.

I didn't ask Hazel Jackson about adjustments directly, but we ended up talking about them anyway. She said that when she got her diagnosis, she didn't run around the organisation shouting about it, but she did tell some key people. She had already had a chat with her line manager about her suspicions of having ADHD, so it wasn't a surprise to those closest to her. Not long after she started at the Woodland Trust, the Covid pandemic hit, and she went from two days working from home, to five. Which she still does now. I asked what it's like working from home full-time, as I found it hard during lockdown. Hazel said that it gives her more flexibility, she can block time out on her calendar to train in the gym, and if she finds she's staring at her computer procrastinating, she can go in the garden or go for a walk. It sounds perfect to me. She adds that it does mean her values and feelings around working practices don't always meet the expectations of others, but as she says to her own team, she doesn't care how she gets to the outcome, or the time that takes, as long as she isn't burning herself out.

I suppose that Hazel is lucky to be able to do this, and as she works at an executive level herself, it's likely that the Woodland Trust has a strong culture of inclusion for neurodivergent employees. Fostering a neuroinclusive culture is one of the most powerful and cost-effective adjustments that can be put in place. A culture where neurodivergent employees can thrive is key. Where implementing adjustments isn't a hassle and people aren't afraid to request them. Where colleagues are accepting and respectful of individual differences. Where the expression of skills and creativity is a positive thing. This can bring wider benefits to an organisation or employer. It can lead to better wellbeing and retention of staff, and from a business perspective, neurodivergent people can be an incredible asset.

As well as systemic adjustments, many practical adjustments can be put in place. James Hankins shared an example from when he was doing his careers guidance qualification that makes me chuckle. The course leaders would leave a pot of playdough on his seat, so he could fiddle with it and thereby aid his concentration. What they did, though, was put a pot on everyone's chair so it was less noticeable. This, as James put it, is genius. He also had no shame in telling me that when he sits in an online meeting, he can only concentrate for 20 minutes, so he has a unique way of focusing. He plays with a LEGO® Batman and a toy tractor. As he says, you must sometimes do whatever you know helps you, however ridiculous it may seem. Making something available for people to manipulate from a sensory perspective, such as a fidget toy, is a common and easy adjustment employers can support. It's something that came up in many conversations I had, especially with interviewees with ADHD.

When I was interviewing Hazel online, I couldn't help but notice how fidgety she was. She then began waving an array of fidget toys she'd been using whilst we were talking that were below the camera's view. A member of the Wildlife Trusts staff said they can use a discreet fidget wristband as a reasonable adjustment. Various people spoke about having to fidget with something when meeting online and the blessing that comes with keeping them out of the line of sight. Whilst discussing the practical side of reasonable adjustments, there's one I must share from Simon Stennet, an RSPB area manager in the south of England. He told me about a colleague with ADHD, who struggles with physical symptoms such as restlessness and fidgeting. Whenever they had a meeting, they had to be walking outdoors. They were unable to focus, process and respond unless they were outside in nature, and the RSPB were supportive of this as an adjustment. I don't think you can better this as far as adjustments go; it's just incredible.

Simon has several adjustments in place for his own ADHD, which all lean into the practical side of work. For example, he uses a standing desk, which is something I periodically use myself and can attest to its usefulness. He also has noise-cancelling headphones, multiple screens to support him with multitasking, and his own office to aid his concentration. Of course, these things require space and money, but the difference they can make to someone's productivity can be huge. The other benefit of Simon having his own working space is for his colleagues, as it means he doesn't disturb anyone when he uses his voice-to-text software. A lot of the people I spoke to who have a diagnosis of dyslexia have been given this sort of software to help them with longer pieces of writing, such as reports, and with general notetaking. Adjustments like this cost money, and to help with this there is the Access to Work scheme, from the Department for Work and Pensions (DWP).

Access to Work is fantastic. It is an employment support programme, where all funding comes from the public purse. Its purpose is to help people with disabilities start and stay in work. There are so many things that can be funded, from practical adjustments like the ones above, to the employment of interpreters or mentors to work alongside you. The scheme can also help with travel arrangements and adaptations, and can support you in advocating for other adjustments, such as your pattern of work, or approaches that support your communication needs within the workplace. To be eligible, you must be living in the UK, over 16, have a diagnosis of a condition that affects your ability to stay in work, and either be in work or about to start. You can go online, check eligibility, and then complete an application form there and then, if your employer consents. I did one for an e-ink paper tablet for work, and some of the hardware that goes with it. The DWP paid for 80 per cent of the cost, and my employer paid the other 20 per cent. The cost is always split but is dealt with on a case-by-case basis.

Another simple but effective adjustment is to collate the approaches that work for individual employees into a document of some description. Most organisations and employers call these 'workplace passports'. Simon showed me around the RSPB's online hub for their reasonable adjustments passports. One of the things that really stood out to me was that their passports aren't led by diagnoses or conditions, instead the RSPB encourage staff members to reflect on challenges they may face in their working role, and things that might mitigate those challenges. I love this approach, as it means that there's no need to be put into a pigeonhole. Someone can just say, 'You know what, I do really struggle to remember things', and then open a discussion with their line manager on what can be put in place to support them. This adds a buffer for people who don't want to disclose anything, or may be exploring, or even unaware of, their neurodivergence. Simon is rightfully proud of the work he's done on this.

Someone else employing exceptionally good practice is Vera Pudilova, who is autistic and works for the Environment Agency as an advisor in communications and engagement. Vera is also a co-chair of the agency's Autism and ADHD network, which has over 1,000 members. Whilst discussing the network, she sent me a document she put together herself, compiling suggestions for workplace adjustments that is particularly geared towards employees with 'autistic and ADHD traits'. This was then made available to the Autism and ADHD network, receiving over 3,000 views. I really like the fact that it's not diagnostic. It is split into sections covering various aspects of work that may require additional support, from online meetings to general communications; there's a lot of detail. Vera wrote it because she wasn't entirely sure what adjustments were widely available, so began collating the strategies in her own workplace passport with those from another 30 people's passports, and some from previous work that she'd done with an autism charity. That was two years ago, and she continues to add to it now. I love the fact that the document is organic, is available to all, and centralises the range of ideas for both the people who implement adjustments and those requesting them.

National Trust ranger Alister Harman doesn't like to ask for a lot, and therefore, is reluctant to make requests for reasonable adjustments. The one thing he does insist on is that everyone accepts that he won't use the same language and mannerisms to engage with people as they might expect from others who aren't neurodivergent. He doesn't want to be masking at work, it's too draining, and as a ranger that's no good as he needs to have his wits about him. He also likes to know what's going on so he can set his expectations accordingly. He accepts that there will always be curveballs in his role, and he has made what he calls his 'Standard Operating Procedure' for dealing with sudden change. Alister believes that honesty is always the best policy and asks for open discussions about planning and decision-making so he can file it away in his brain, process it, and therefore not be in shock when changes come around. There's a secondary benefit for Alister when he knows what's happening as it gives him something to attempt conversation with. What's striking is that Alister isn't asking for anything other than clarity and openness.

These are simple approaches to implement. They are also free, which makes for happy budget-holders. But these attitudinal changes will always be the most powerful adjustments. This usually starts with educating all levels of an organisation about neurodiversity, and showing a commitment to doing so. Another simple step towards a neuroinclusive culture might be for staff of any seniority to share their neurodivergence with others and openly discuss it. Of course, they must be comfortable in doing this, and it mustn't be done in a tokenistic way. Setting up a staff neurodiversity network, or networks for specific conditions, can be an effective way of showing dedication towards inclusion. I started to do this while working at a multi-academy trust, but encountered some challenges with the IT department, who flagged my channel titled 'HR and employment issues'. This led me to reflect on the organisation's culture and realise that it wasn't as neuroinclusive as it aimed to be. However, there are plenty of adjustments mentioned in this chapter that you can consider, many of which are also budget-friendly.

An anonymous contributor gave the idea of workplace adjustments a fitting analogy. They said that adjustments are as much about working with people and listening to their needs as they are about implementing new protocols. They likened this to a metaphor involving different plant species. Some plant species are common and can be successful in the hardest of conditions, whereas others require more specialist conditions to flourish. To me this is what reasonable adjustments are all about, and as a line manager myself, I always work alongside my colleagues to help identify what might enable them to grow professionally. On deeper reflection, I see myself as an inclusive leader, embedding structure, but allowing flexibility, harnessing strengths and supporting colleagues with individual issues as they arise. However, the sad truth is that I'm only able to do this because of some of the negative management approaches I've been on the receiving end of during my own career. Ultimately, it doesn't take much to be supportive and offer some empathy. I firmly believe that there should be some kind of mandatory neurodiversity awareness training for everyone who has the responsibility of managing others.

When I step back and reflect, I can't help but think that the biggest adjustment of all has been staring back at me all along. Being outside. So many of the roles in conservation involve spending time outdoors, and it is widely understood what the benefits of this can be, not only for neurodivergent people, but for anyone. When I checked over my notes, I found there were no contributors working in outdoor roles and requiring adjustments for that element of their job. The tweaks came when human and social interactions had to take place, in whatever form that might be. In short, it's the people, the administrative tasks and sharing information that cause the most issues for neurodivergent people. There's a degree of irony that in a sector with a focus on the natural environment, it's the human one that presents us with challenges. This is true even when it comes to accessing natural spaces, as we humans are the ones that take them away, or refuse entry. Also, remember that adjustments happen when someone commences or is already in employment, and whilst of course that's positive, it doesn't address the inequity of access to the conservation sector in general.

Something that's clearly moving in a positive direction is the overarching desire to make workplaces as accessible as possible, especially for people who are neurodivergent. Reasonable adjustments are the foundation of this, and it has been reassuring to be able to share so many positive experiences of these for so many people. As we found out earlier, they don't always happen, and if I'm brutally honest, it would have been easy to focus on the lack of accessibility in this chapter, if not the entire book. However, what use is a scathing overview of neurodivergence in the conservation sector when you can celebrate it instead?

We'll be heading next into the realm of the specific employers in the sector, the larger conservation organisations such as the RSPB and the Environment Agency, many of which are household names.

CHAPTER TEN
Peeking over the fence to see what next door are up to

Nature related NGOs

If you're in or around the conservation sector, you will have heard of the term 'NGOs', which stands for non-governmental organisations. These are not-for-profit organisations who don't receive any funding from the government, therefore they do their own fundraising. This happens in many ways, from membership fees and street canvassing to receiving legacy payments. Being reliant on generating income means that these organisations must constantly evolve, jump on and off bandwagons, and keep up to date with what is engaging people across multiple platforms. This is why they employ people to work intensively on fundraising, campaigning and communications. At a time when the cost of living is so high, NGOs have to work particularly hard to be innovative and creative, offer value for money, and remain relevant. When you see it written like this, you realise what a mammoth task this must be, and the huge level of thought that must go into it, not to mention the cost. It harks back to what I've said a few times in this book now, that to conserve nature we need people, but to engage those people, we need other people to facilitate that engagement. It is far more complex than it first appears.

NGOs are vast. They are made up of lots of different departments and functions, employing a wide range of people. Those in conservation often own and manage sites of special scientific interest, nature reserves and pockets of land all over the country, many of which are accessible to the public. The work of a conservation NGO may involve practical conservation, such as managing their sites to preserve, protect and restore them. Their work may involve ecological consultancy and research, especially on their sites, but they also work with landowners to better manage their areas of land. They advocate for nature and lobby the government, usually through campaigns that engage the public to support their causes, such as the banning of a neonicotinoid pesticide harmful to bees. They target everyone, from children to older people, through every channel imaginable. They also promote what are known as citizen-science initiatives, encouraging us to join them in monitoring species nationally, such as through counting our garden birds. Conservation NGOs are remarkably clever in a system sense, in the way they are adaptable and responsive, retaining an appeal to a diverse spread of people.

What's great about these larger organisations, and helpful for me, is that thanks to their sizable workforces, they must take neurodivergence seriously, as it's statistically impossible for them not to have neurodivergent staff. This means that somewhere, there'll be someone with the overall responsibility for equity, diversity and inclusion, usually referred to as EDI or DEI (but thankfully never DIE), and this is often a senior staff member. Depending on the level of commitment to EDI and the funding available, some NGOs will have an entire team working in this area.

Most conservation NGOs are charities overseen by the charity commission. This means they must operate for public benefit and work towards their own charitable objectives. It is not a legal requirement for a charity to report on EDI, however it is a recommendation in the guidance on charity governance, and most charities will detail their approaches somewhere, even if it's not in their annual reporting. At the very least, hidden somewhere online, a commitment to EDI will be worded into a policy or mission statement. It will be something glossy, corporate and well made.

The largest conservation charity in the UK is the RSPB and their employees have already featured throughout this book. The society came about in the late 1800s to combat the use of feathers in the fashion industry, and over time it has grown to more than 1.2 million members and more than 2,000 employees. The RSPB is a machine. It has so many strings to its proverbial bow, all focused on its overall mission to protect wildlife in the UK and around the world. I had to do a little digging on the RSPB website to find out about EDI, but a policy sits in the 'how we are run' section under 'key management policies'. It seems legitimate enough to my layman's eyes, but with no specific mention of neurodiversity. I type various words pertaining to neurodivergence into the site's search bar, but surprisingly, nothing comes up. I cast the net wider and search for the same words and 'RSPB' on an internet search engine but find very little information.

In their key management policy, and in an article on race equality, the RSPB has written extensively about their drive towards a more diverse staff team. The focus of this is, rightfully, on ethnic diversity, but semantically, they write about 'people' and 'all', which translates to all members of society, and therefore includes neurodivergent people too.

However, in the RSPB's 2021–2022 annual report, not only is there a section sharing the recruitment of a specific EDI team, but there is also a direct mention of the RSPB affinity groups (their staff networks), including some neurodiversity groups for raising awareness on how to better support and engage neurodivergent people, through a series of talks and workshops. There's also a specific quote from Simon Stennet, who, in addition to being an RSPB area manager, also works half a day a week in the EDI team. In the quote, he extols the benefits of nature for autistic people and people with ADHD, as well as acknowledging that he has ADHD. I can't express just how empowering it is to see this in the annual report of such a large and well-known organisation.

Simon became an incredible source of information about neurodivergence at the RSPB, and he also ended up being an ally of the book. He was unable to share specific figures on neurodivergence, so gave me his own estimate, which comes from the work he has been doing on neurodiversity across the society. He suggested that up to 30 per cent of the RSPB workforce, possibly more, are neurodivergent, although there will be many people who are simply unaware or haven't got a diagnosis. He feels that any workforce surveys won't necessarily be representative of true figures, and this is largely because in wider society there's still a huge lack of awareness of neurodivergence. Whenever Simon does any presentations on neurodiversity awareness, at the start he'll always ask if anyone identifies as neurodivergent through an anonymous questionnaire. Afterwards, he does this again, and the figure is always higher. This really does demonstrate how having open conversations about neurodivergence can help other people to recognise it in themselves, and ultimately, choose to seek advice and support.

Simon was a great person to talk to about reasonable adjustments, as I think it's fair to say that it's his special interest. He does feel like the RSPB has a lot of work to do in this area, but loves being able to take on a key role in driving this forward within the organisation. He says that embedding the principle of reasonable adjustments is a high priority for the RSPB in terms of EDI, and its EDI lead is pushing very hard to integrate reasonable adjustment passports into HR processes. He said there are lots of adjustments built into general ways of working that aren't explicitly formal; things such as flexible working, additional breaks, ensuring that meetings have a 10-minute pause each hour to break them up and having no formal dress code, which is excellent for reducing some of the sensory issues that formal work attire can cause.

One of the main things Simon and the EDI team have been working on is the development of their fantastic 'reasonable adjustment hub', with a whole section of reasonable adjustments specifically for supporting neurodivergent colleagues. The hub is accessible to all staff through an internal intranet. It contains guidance on neurodiversity, on how to complete reasonable adjustment passports, and a lot of information on the challenges employees may face and what can be put in place to help with these. These are under a series of headings, which are accessible and easy to navigate. As he showed me, I interrupted to tell him just how accessible it was. From font size to layout, it was very impressive. He said that this was always the intent, and you can feel it in the way it operates. Simon is keen that the passports are led by challenges and not by diagnoses, as people don't fit into pigeonholes and are in what he calls 'a state of balance and flux'. Another nice touch is that there is guidance for both employees and line managers, but neither is hidden from the other, so expectations are transparent. The hub also links to the various employee networks at the RSPB, including the ADHD network that Simon leads which has just over 100 members, and a new neurodivergent families network, where parents, partners and carers of neurodivergent children can share experiences and support each other.

Simon describes the ADHD network page as a kind of corporate social media, where people can chat, interact and advocate for each other. There's also a monthly 'ADHD social' online meet, which strikes me as an excellent idea. So too does something that Simon talked me through, which is the use of 'accountability buddies' or 'body doubling'. He told me about research that shows that if you've got ADHD and you're struggling with procrastination and motivation, it can make a huge difference to have someone with you in the room or holding you to account. He described the scenario of being in an office and wandering off-task. Often the pressures and distractions of having people around you, or engaging with you, can pull you back on-task. This has been somewhat lost since Covid, with more people working from home. Simon was able to send out a single meeting invite to everyone in the ADHD network, which once accepted, allowed the chat to roll in the background. If anyone felt they might benefit from someone to co-work with, or to hold them accountable and be 'in the room', they could ask if anyone was free to work together, virtually. I genuinely think the whole idea is genius.

In terms of overall employment experiences as neurodivergent people, most people I spoke to said that this was often completely dependent on the attitude of their line manager. Although people's experiences were generally positive, there was a consensus that more could be done to improve knowledge and understanding of specific differences. This happens with time, with training, and with awareness, which I know are areas that the RSPB is focusing on. Everyone I spoke to there was positive about the affinity group networks, and the support, advice and community that they get from them. Simon describes these as a 'ground-up' movement, and I like the almost activist overtones in these words. It feels like a voice is being given to those who don't always get the opportunity to have one. In a general sense, it feels like the RSPB's EDI team are working tirelessly to improve things, and Simon says that awareness of neurodiversity across the RSPB has risen dramatically in the last few years, as it also has across society. In a constantly evolving landscape, it's great to see such a large organisation adapting and learning how to meet the needs of its staff and supporters.

Next up is the Wildlife Trusts, which are made up of 46 individual charities around the UK, boasting more than 900,000 members, a massive 35,000 volunteers, and more than 3,000 paid staff members. Each separate Wildlife Trust is a local independent charity with its own constitution, but all sit under the collective charitable umbrella of the Royal Society of Wildlife Trusts (RSWT), operating since 1912. The local Wildlife Trusts tend to cover a county or area, whereas the RSWT acts more as a collective advisory and lobbying voice, representing all of them. For example, there are many sites in Norfolk that are run by the Norfolk Wildlife Trust. As well as practical conservation, they also do some great outreach work; at their Cley Marshes site, for instance, they have an all-year calendar of activities and events. The Wildlife Trusts are a prominent and active group of organisations, managing many sites around the country, with an aim to both conserve nature and connect people with it. It seems fair to assume that with such a diverse offering, the Wildlife Trusts will champion diversity and have a strong culture of inclusion. From information available in the public domain, this appears to be the case.

The Wildlife Trusts publish an annual diversity report, which is an insightful and accessible document. The pervading message in all their EDI information is that they still have huge amounts of work to do to be truly inclusive. As an organisation, they have made their own framework, Wild About Inclusion, but I was unable to find the detail of this anywhere. As I did with the RSPB, I sent some questions to the media team, who connected me with the Trusts' strategic lead for EDI, who was more than happy to engage with me. I did receive a response via email, but there was no offer of a chat or a meeting, which was a shame. The answers were brief, but I'm aware of the fact that an EDI lead at any large organisation is going to have multiple plates to spin, so it wasn't an issue. I found their latest staff EDI survey online, and as the questions rarely ask if you're neurodivergent, there was no specific data on this. However, 27.8 per cent of the staff that gave a response to the latest survey consider themselves to have at least one disability. They also don't collect this data for their vast volunteer workforce, either, but have been working on how this can be done in future.

The diversity report details six staff networks, two of which are pertinent for neurodivergent people: 'Nature for All', which is for any staff member who consider themselves to have a disability, and 'Nature in Mind', a network for staff experiencing poor mental health, which can intersect with neurodivergence. I did ask if I could speak to network leaders, and the EDI lead tried to set this up. One of the network leaders did engage with me, but as is so often the case when two neurodivergent people try to make plans, it didn't go any further than a few emails. One member of staff told me that Nature for All has a lower sign-up rate than some other staff groups and wonders if this is due to stigma around declaring a disability, which may well be the case. None of the organisations I spoke with has a disability network membership figure that reflects their declaration rate. Either way, it seemed like a missed opportunity not to speak with anyone in the networks – particularly to understand senior-level representation and their role in driving change. That said, for those willing to look, plenty of information is available.

The EDI lead told me that the Wildlife Trusts are implementing an accessibility passport scheme, giving staff a platform to share what their good and bad days are like, to request any support they may require, and ask for any reasonable adjustments they might wish to explore. In a fine example of inclusive practice, a member of staff I spoke to was given the opportunity to meet with HR and look through some prototype passports. A stand-out detail for them was the idea of sharing what a 'good' and 'bad' day might look like, as they felt that the symptoms of many hidden disabilities can fluctuate, and on some days, they may be experiencing more issues than on others. Adjustments are on a case-by-case basis, and are the remit of the local Trust. Some examples include flexible working, consolidation of hours, changes in working location, additional time to complete tasks, and permission to keep cameras off during online calls. One member of staff, who has a background in EDI, told me that through being quite confident in asking for adjustments, they can work very flexibly, managing their own time and sometimes even having 'work from bed days' for days where they're recovering from overwhelm or sensory overload.

I spoke to a senior staff member at a Wildlife Trust to find out if individual Trusts lead their own EDI work. I discovered that each Trust is autonomous and makes their own decisions, including how to deliver outcomes on EDI. They echo the EDI lead's comment that EDI has become a major focus, receiving significant investment in recent years. EDI is now a regular discussion topic, but because it's relatively new, training and communications can still seem quite generic. I was then told that EDI topics tend to reflect whatever is in the public discourse at the time, and discussions around neurodivergence tend to focus on this too. Of course, there could be more substance and depth, but for neurodivergence to even have a presence is a positive thing, and I do think that generic themes are the entry point for most large organisations. They were abundantly clear with me that the Wildlife Trusts' EDI team work tirelessly to raise awareness, and this is already having positive impacts.

As an example, the senior staff member mentioned the EDI team's bite-size 60-second videos, raising awareness of topical themes and starting conversations between colleagues. I recognised that this initiative may slightly raise organisational levels of awareness, but with each Trust delivering EDI differently and focussing on different topics, I'm unsure if this broad support will alter long-held stereotypes that can often underpin protected characteristics. The senior staff member beautifully described how they perceive much of the delivery of organisational EDI work as 'peeking over the fence to see what next door are up to, then trying to keep up with the Jones's, rather than thinking about what they should deliver and why.' Essentially, this approach could undermine both local needs and wider diversity, rather than supporting and championing the true causes. They mentioned that there has always been a strong focus on diversity within individual Trusts and this has encouraged a widespread culture of acceptance within the organisation. However, I do wonder if this acceptance, the local knowledge of individual staff, and the diversity of volunteers, means that Trusts feel like much safer spaces than many other workplaces. This isn't a bad thing at all, but I suppose it could make it harder for people to fly the nest in fear of not being able to find another safe place to land.

I think the biggest issue of localised autonomy is that it's incredibly difficult to embed an organisational culture and implement change, as everyone sits in their silos doing things 'their' way. Some of the staff I spoke to said that the central EDI work of the Trust was incredibly positive, but that when it gets down to grassroots level, they often end up facilitating their own adjustments and managing their own neurodivergent needs, on top of their working roles. Conversely, another employee said that the organisation and its staff are very inclusive, noting that their manager had recently done some training in 'neurodiversity for community engagement', which they felt could work just as well for their neurodivergent colleagues. I feel like this disparity within individual experiences of management can be a huge barrier, and it's positive to see that one of the Trusts' diversity outcomes is to improve their diverse and inclusive leadership. In the diversity report, there is a mention of providing 'high value' EDI training, which reminded me of my suggestion of mandatory neurodiversity awareness training. Why couldn't something like that be sector-specific to conservation? I also suggest to them about how much I would love to create a cross-organisation neurodiversity action group as a way of uniting best practices.

The last organisation I investigated was the National Trust, which has existed since 1895 and is now Europe's largest conservation charity. The National Trust protects and shares a range of places – from stately homes, castles, gardens and parks to entire sections of coastline. It boasts just shy of six million members, around 7,600 paid staff and 44,000 volunteers. With such a huge workforce, it's impossible for EDI to not be on its agenda, but it proved difficult to get any meaningful information. As with all large organisations, the gatekeeping was intense, and I was just a random person asking for data. Eventually the Trust told me it currently doesn't share equalities monitoring data other than the gender pay gap, which is in its annual report, but it has been considering expanding data reporting to other areas, including ethnicity and disability. However, along with the other two 'big guns', the National Trust has put EDI at the forefront of its strategic vision. In its 2020–2025 strategy, 'For everyone, for ever', the Trust makes a commitment to 'be an inclusive, welcoming and sustainable organisation' that values the diversity of its people and supporters.

This is driven by its EDI framework, 'Everyone Welcome', which has its own team and acts as a best-practice umbrella across the entire organisation. There's a strong focus on accessibility, including disability and socio-economic access to the places it conserves. Two of the celebrated achievements in the Trust's most recent annual report reflect this focus: investing £3 million to improve accessibility to its places, and overhauling its recruitment processes to reach a wider diversity of job applicants. The latter has been done by using some approaches that highlight strengths. There are three inclusion networks, one of which, WorkAbility, focuses on staff who identify as having one or more disabilities. The co-chairs of the network are Lavinia Bramwell and Heather Smith, and both were happy to contribute to this chapter. They began by informing me that the network has been around since the summer of 2020, and came about when there were already two inclusion networks, one for race equity, and one for LGBTQ+ people, but it was felt that there was also a need for one for colleagues with a disability. The three networks form an 'inclusion council', which meets thrice-yearly with senior leaders and executive sponsors, including the director-general of the Trust.

I asked what they perceived the function of the network to be, and they said that they provide a 'safe space for disabled and neurodivergent staff to unite and support each other.' They also educate executive leaders on the barriers that people face in the workplace, and advocate and push for changes to make working at the National Trust a positive experience. Their initial work had a strong focus on reasonable adjustments, and as the network has grown, their work has expanded through tiers of management, as they look towards improving the inclusive culture of the Trust. Their vision for the future is one where 'disabled and neurodivergent people can bring their whole selves to work and receive appreciation for the skills and expertise they bring to the workplace.' They want to see the removal of barriers to ensure people can fully contribute, and for it to be recognised that diversity of thought can bring fresh exciting ideas. This isn't a pipedream either, as the staff members from the National Trust who I spoke to about this book were incredibly positive, although I will say that three of these were people who had already spoken openly about their neurodivergence, either on other platforms, or as celebrated case studies for the Trust.

Ranger Alister Harman said that his National Trust managers will openly talk about his autism with him and have been great about listening to and discussing his thoughts. He described them as professionals who are good at their jobs, and added that he doesn't feel like he's constantly struggling against the tide as he understands their expectations of him. Michael Howard also praised his manager, saying that they are hugely supportive, wants to get the best out of their diverse team, and understands the adjustments their staff need. Michael shared some of his own adjustments and others he's seen around the Trust, such as flexible working arrangements and a focus on individual communication methods. In his office, they now have caller ID on their phones, as not knowing who's calling can cause him high levels of anxiety. He described how some larger meetings now have fidget toys on the tables and that more thought is given to venue choices. He also mentioned how, similarly to those in the RSPB, managers are actively looking to implement body doubling for staff who might need it.

Tracey Churcher, who is a general manager at the National Trust, also has a supportive line manager, who allows her to lead with passion and trusts her judgement, which is especially important to her as she struggles with rejection sensitive dysphoria, also known as RSD. This is a common aspect of the ADHD profile, where someone experiences extreme emotional sensitivity at rejection from people important to them. This bleeds into her management style, and she describes her focus as 'present/future', preferring to discuss things as they happen rather than ruminating on the past. She feels like her approach means her staff know that she wants what's best for them as individuals, and that being open about her own differences creates a circle of trust.

Adjustments-wise, Tracey is all over it. She has even arranged for a car to be bought for a staff member with a physical disability, which other volunteers drive for them at work, the return being the fresh perspectives on accessibility and inclusion that this colleague brings. Tracey's Purbeck site has also installed Makaton signs (an augmentative and alternative communication system using signs and symbols alongside speech and words), provided walking poles to help people access higher areas, set up virtual tours on tablet computers, and had a Changing Places accessible toilet put in place. Tracey says that her team are 'ahead of the curve' with their work on accessibility, and she is immensely proud of this.

A significant milestone for EDI in the National Trust was its first WorkAbility conference, which took place in Cheshire in 2023. It took months for Heather and Lavinia to plan, and it was just for network members, either in person or online. 47 people went to the venue, and 30 attended virtually. It was very much about the network, sharing personal stories and connecting. So much thought went into it. Heather and Lavinia chose a venue that could cater for a range of dietary requirements, had an accessible lift, had various rooms to choose from (they went for one with a lower ceiling to improve acoustics), and even had an accessible bus from the car park to the main building. The level of detail was immense. Expectations for engagement in sessions were clear and minimal, quiet spaces were available, and timings were concise and engaging. There were mental-health first aiders on site, a hearing loop, captions on all electronic visuals and fidget toys on all tables, which were a massive hit. The feedback was incredibly positive, and it didn't take much for them to start planning for their second conference in 2024.

The 2024 conference was themed around career development, and over 100 people went, along with delegates from WorkAbility's 'allies', people from external organisations tackling the barriers to inclusion that they face themselves. The Trust had learnt from the first conference that a full day was too much for most, so they split the 2024 conference over two days. On the first day, attendees met their new steering group leaders, heard from a neurodivergent senior leader about their own strengths and challenges, and had presentations from their allies. The second day was focused on the internal workings at the Trust, discussing various themes such as equity versus equality, changes to recruitment, reasonable adjustments, and Access to Work. The conferences have been so successful that the WorkAbility team have now put together some pioneering guidance for other organisations on how to run inclusive and accessible conferences. Lavinia is rightfully proud of how much the network has grown, in both numbers and confidence. People trust them both inside and outside the organisation, and this helps them to drive change and share best practice.

As Tracey said to me, the original aim of the National Trust's founder, Octavia Hill, was to retain access to nature. After the Second World War, saving our failing great houses became the focus of the Trust. Now it's nature and people that need the Trust, and in Tracey's opinion, that's where they're heading. It was refreshing to hear about and be able to share some of the excellent EDI practice that's happening in the conservation sector. It's evident that the sector's leaders have a genuine investment in neurodivergence and recognise that their sector naturally attracts people who think differently and bring with them a wealth of skills. It makes sense for them to adjust and adapt to make the employment experiences of these people as positive as possible. Of course, this reminds us that, ultimately, biodiversity needs neurodiversity. It isn't just the three NGOs in this chapter that account for the conservation sector; there are a plethora of smaller organisations and charities too. And there are also a few more massive machines that fall into a completely different category. A spectral overlord that I'm fearful of approaching. The government.

CHAPTER ELEVEN
A rose-tinted perspective on the use of the infographic

Government agencies

There was never a plan to speak to the governmental side of the conservation sector. Mainly because I thought they wouldn't engage. However, following a callout on social media, I was contacted by someone from Natural England, who sent me a wealth of information about its approaches to EDI and neurodivergence. At the time, I couldn't work out where it fitted into the book, so it went in an 'extra bits' folder and into the ether. A year later, following another callout, an employee of the Environment Agency got in touch, offering to share my request in a staff dyslexia network. The response was incredible, enough for a chapter, and after a lightbulb moment, I went into 'extra bits' and began to add information about Natural England too. I quickly learnt that public sector organisations have a legal obligation to report on equality and diversity as part of the Equality Act, under what's known as the Public Sector Equality Duty. This is a statutory duty applying to all public authorities and bodies carrying out public duties. It ensures that these organisations consider how their functions will affect people with different protected characteristics.

Public authorities and public bodies must 'eliminate unlawful discrimination, harassment, victimisation and any other unlawful conduct prohibited by the act', they must 'advance equality of opportunity between people who share and people who do not share a relevant protected characteristic', and they must 'foster good relations between people who share and people who do not share a relevant protected characteristic.' Government guidance states that compliance with the general duty 'involves consciously thinking about the equality aims while making decisions.' There is no specific expectation or guidance on how to record and report on this conscious thinking while decision making, but there is guidance for the three specific duties. There's a suggestion that a team can work on ensuring compliance with them, and depending on the size of the organisation, the expectation is that they may have to publish one or more equality objectives at least every four years, annual gender pay-gap data, and sometimes, annual information on the organisation's compliance with the general duty. What this means in principle is that most of the organisations I'd be speaking to must, in some way, share EDI data.

Natural England and the Environment Agency are 'arm's length bodies' of Defra, the government department with responsibility for improving and protecting the environment, and supporting the UK's farming and fishing industries. This is a broad description of an incredibly wide remit, and doesn't do justice to the reality of their work. Their departmental outcomes range from reducing emissions via animal welfare, to marine conservation, to managing flooding and erosion. Defra only covers England, but employs over 10,000 people, which to me is mind-blowing. They also work with 34 other agencies and public bodies. I won't list them all, but some you may recognise are the Forestry Commission, Royal Botanic Gardens Kew, the Broads Authority, nine different national park authorities, and of course, Natural England and the Environment Agency.

I'll begin with the organisation that got in touch with me all that time ago, Natural England. It describes itself as the government's adviser for the natural environment in England. The 2006 Natural Environment and Rural Communities Act was the catalyst for its formation, dissolving the Countryside Agency and English Nature to form a new body, Natural England, whose purpose was set out in this act of parliament and remains the same today, 'To ensure that the natural environment is conserved, enhanced and managed for the benefit of present and future generations, thereby contributing to sustainable development.' This is an enormous remit, again, and I can't help but think that as an organisation, it must be in a constant state of treading water. Its current priorities cover many areas, a few examples of which are the development of green infrastructure, connecting people with nature, and working with various partners on nature recovery. The sheer vastness of work explains why Natural England employs close to 3,000 staff across the country.

That's a large workforce, and, as with all other organisations, there are going to be neurodivergent employees. So what is Natural England doing to support and recognise these people? Like everyone else who falls under the umbrella of Defra, it adheres to the department's EDI strategy. This sets out a vision for creating a more diverse and inclusive family of organisations within Defra with strategic objectives around culture, workforce diversity, confidence in addressing EDI challenges, and sharing good practice and progress in these areas. It also publishes its actions and measures as part of the strategy, and although direct and corporate in their presentation, it's evident that as a department, it takes it all seriously. It commits to a wide range of activities to benefit all their employees. This includes pledging to engage with their staff networks, of which there is a neurodiversity-specific one, to equip leaders and managers with the knowledge and skills to drive an inclusive culture, to overhaul their recruitment practices to build a more diverse workforce, to improve their provision of reasonable adjustments, to get better at responding to changing EDI landscapes and work in partnership to do this, and, most importantly, to report on this and form a stronger evidence base.

Natural England has its own EDI strategy, as well as Defra's. In its organisational action plan, it aims to invest in its people, ensuring it is growing a diverse organisation and that its people have the skills and confidence to realise their potential. Under this sits the programme 'Connecting People with Nature', which aims to tackle barriers to nature and address the lack of diversity in the sector and Natural England's staff body. I couldn't find any progress reporting on this specific action plan, but as it covers five years, ending in 2025, it's fair to assume that publicly available reporting will appear after that. Annual reporting does happen, but internally to its board, and externally to Defra. This is where my early contact comes back into play. Step up Paul Hinds. Paul is Natural England's principal adviser on public engagement for nature and society. I couldn't have wished for a better person to speak to about the work Natural England is doing on EDI, neurodiversity and engaging people, and what's more, Paul has ADHD too!

Paul was honest about the fact that EDI can be seen as more of a process and doesn't necessarily account for individual needs. To some at senior level, if the process is in place and is in action, then EDI has been addressed. But as we know, it doesn't work like that. One of Natural England's strategic aims is to increase the diversity of its workforce, with neurodiversity particularly lacking at senior leadership level, according to Paul. His role involves a lot of partnership work. If this is EDI-focused, then it tends to be under a broader umbrella of EDI, rather than focusing on specific characteristics. This means that a lot of external engagement is within a framing of general 'inclusion'. We know that drilling down into specifics is key, but this costs money and resources, so it doesn't always fit in with corporate approaches. I'm not under any illusions regarding this. Paul speaks of working in partnership with other public bodies, NGOs such as the RSPB, and representatives of community organisations. He says that partner meetings are usually run in a formal way, and Natural England often takes on a secretarial role. As they're mainly voluntary to attend, diversity can be an issue, somewhat ironically, at a round-table event on diversity. However, Natural England now covers attendees' costs where relevant, which seems to be facilitating an increase in the diversity of voices at such events.

Paul described the Defra employee networks to me as 'listening circles', which I like. The networks don't, however, provide opportunities to directly engage with senior leaders, as the lack of diversity at that level also means there's no senior representation in the networks themselves, which is a shame. This felt like the ideal time to source someone in a senior position at Natural England to gather their perspective and oversight. I was able to arrange and eventually meet online with Natural England's director of people, James Diamond. He was open with me from the beginning of our chat that, although Natural England does some great work around neurodivergence, there's a lot more it could do. Like most organisations, it doesn't specifically collect data on it, but its overall EDI declaration rate is a whopping 89 per cent of employees, of which 18 per cent declare as having a disability, up from 15 per cent two years ago. James is also the 'senior champion' of Natural England's disability staff network, and out of interest I asked him if he identified as having one himself, and he does. He is rightfully proud of this representation and believes that it helps staff to feel more confident in disclosing their own disabilities, and I agree.

We went on to discuss the importance of creating an inclusive culture through demonstrating openness and honesty at the highest echelons of leadership. He shared an example where a member of staff in his team recently got an autism diagnosis and felt comfortable enough to inform him immediately, without any concern for their wellbeing at work, or for their career. He also shared that it's the staff that shape any work on neurodivergence, by continuing to challenge leaders and raise awareness. James said that he actively encourages challenge, as it's the only way the organisation moves forward. It was so powerful and refreshing to hear this, and he added that Natural England has begun rolling out a 'reverse mentoring' scheme, where senior leaders, including its chief executive, receive mentoring from representatives in its disability and race networks. The idea is that this will help to grow senior leaders' understanding, insight and engagement. This demonstrates that Natural England acknowledges that upskilling leaders around EDI is a vital part of embedding an inclusive culture. We moved on to discussing adjustments for staff, and he described some classic examples that mirror those seen in other organisations. It's positive that there's a kind of 'blanket' expectation of adjustments now.

However, James raised an important point, that adjustments and attitudes largely rest on the line-management experience that people receive on an individual basis. This is why another area of improvement that James identifies is ensuring that the support staff get is consistently good across all teams and managers. He knows that Natural England's policies are robust and they can demonstrate good practice, but that equally it needs to keep on supporting managers. This also came up when I spoke with Paul, and he said that all Natural England employees must complete an online training module on 'civil service expectations', which covers EDI. He added that all people managers complete a one-day training course on leading inclusive teams, and a half-day course on inclusive disability management. However, and this is my own take, there will always be managers in any workplace who see such training as a hoop to jump through, or a tick-box exercise. These courses can be a great starting point, providing an overview, albeit with a scant level of detail. I say this from experience, and nothing beats getting to know your colleagues' differences on an individual level.

As I've also come to expect, Natural England has a workplace passport scheme, and the staff I speak to all have them. Paul noted that they work well when a line manager has a good understanding of an individual's needs and works with them daily. There has been a push to have these in place, which is understandable from the perspective of both employer and employee, as they can help manage and mitigate any issues before escalation. Paul shares his with any new colleagues he'll be working with as it saves having to explain and often re-justify why he works in a certain way. I asked Paul if the uptake of passports is good, and he said it is, but there will always be colleagues who are reluctant as they perceive it may be a career block for them. This echoes James's sentiments that there will always be improvements to be made regarding EDI. As James rightfully said, certain conditions, and working environments, can always present the possibility of behaviour that challenges colleagues. This reminds me of the classic example of people assuming that autistic colleagues are rude because of how they communicate socially with others. Educating others about the nuances of neurodivergence will always be paramount.

Inez Williams-King, who we met earlier, also works as a senior landscape advisor within Natural England's Landscape, Heritage and Geodiversity Team, and has done for two years. She described her experience of being a neurodivergent staff member at Natural England in glowing terms. It began with adjustments at the interview stage, receiving some example questions in advance so that she could prepare notes. She shared her email signature, which reads:

> *My apologies if there are any spelling or grammar mistakes or confusion with my email, I have dyslexia. Please understand I do my best to reduce these errors and if you have any questions, please do call me and I am happy to explain my email further.*

It's such a simple but effective way to communicate your needs in a formal, yet approachable manner. Overall, Inez feels that there's an active push in Natural England to increase awareness about neurodivergence across colleagues of all levels and described a 'general kindness' in the organisational culture that allows individuality to flourish. She also shared some of the practical adjustments in place for her dyslexia, like having permission to record and transcribe meetings, and having access to various pieces of software to support her work.

Interestingly, a few weeks after the 2024 UK general election and the change from a Conservative to Labour government, Natural England put out a new action plan, covering the year between 2024 and 2025. Although workforce diversity remains a key priority, it felt like a weaker focus semantically. For me, as an outsider, with only basic ecological knowledge, it felt like they'd been told to refine their strategic aims to be less about people and more about the environment. To be clear, this is just my own observation. I don't understand the machinations of being a governmental organisation, nor is it particularly pertinent to this book, but it must be complex and probably quite taxing to be at the behest of a governmental department. I wonder just how much of the identity of each individual organisation dissipates into the policies, procedures and processes of the overseer. That said, my original discussions with some of the staff and leaders at Natural England felt positive, and demonstrated that it was striving to create an inclusive culture. It remains to be seen if the change in government impacts the entire organisation in the long term, as it certainly seems to have had an impact on its short-term strategic direction.

Now, back to the social-media post that was the tipping point for this chapter, the one that got the Environment Agency 'in' and set the tone. At times, researching the distinction between Natural England and the Environment Agency felt like a bit of a feckless task. Eventually I found a report from 2013, which came about at a time when a proposal to merge the Environment Agency and Natural England was on the table. In the end, the decision was to keep them separate, with different purposes and functions. The overall vision of the Environment Agency is to 'protect and enhance the environment as a whole and contribute to sustainable development'. It has responsibility for reducing the risks of flooding, for people and properties, alongside ensuring there's enough water for people and wildlife. It also protects and improves air, land and water quality, with responsibility for applying industry-wide standards to facilitate this. Furthermore, it works with the emergency services to prepare and respond to incidents, as well as supporting any recovery operations after.

On the equality and diversity section of their website, the Environment Agency commits to 'promoting equality and diversity' in all it does, to regularly publish its equality objectives, and to report on how it is meeting them. Across several strategic documents, it reports that a high percentage of its workforce feels it respects individual differences and upholds its commitment to EDI. Of course, as part of Defra, it adheres to the specific actions and objectives of the department, but, like Natural England, it also has its own systems in place. My first impression of the Environment Agency's own EDI objectives was that they were quite wordy, and to be honest, it was a bit of a trudge to get through them, let alone process the content. There are lots of statistics and references, which I understood the pertinence of, but I did feel it could be made more accessible. The crux of what the organisation is striving for sits in four strategic objectives. In summary, these are to build and develop an inclusive and respectful culture, to increase the diversity of their workforce, to ensure equity of opportunity for all, and to increase its ability to protect and improve the environment for all communities.

It also lists some organisational priorities, one of which is to ensure that its employees have the 'right' reasonable adjustments in place. There are also some actions it pledges to take, which stood out as relevant for this book. Increasing the EDI knowledge of line managers is one, as is increasing the uptake and implementation of employee passports and thus, reasonable adjustments. A visual would have been a great way to represent this data, perhaps through infographics or diagrams. In the end, I found the most interesting snippet of information for this book in yet another report: 'EA2025 creating a better place'. This is an overarching outline of its organisational plans, and as well as the corporate discussion on enhancing diversity, there's this nugget of semantic gold. It reads: 'We will continue to need people who understand the urgency of climate change and have the knowledge, skills and enthusiasm to tackle it.' If you've been paying attention, you'll know that we neurodivergent people have this in abundance. This is them. This is us. If that sentence was in a person specification for a job, all my contributors would be able to tick the proverbial box.

After that initial shoutout, when the member of staff, Sophie Tumber, kindly put my request in the Environment Agency's 'Dyslexia Plus' network, she also sent an email to an EDI mailbox, which was seen by Mikael Chaudary, an EDI adviser for people and change at the Environment Agency. He got in touch with me, and eventually we met online for an interview. I was keen to hear his perspective of the Environment Agency's EDI work. I sent him my questions beforehand so he knew what to expect, and his opening gambit, somewhat disappointingly, was to tell me that he was unable to share disability data with me unless I submitted a freedom of information request. I had thought this may be the case with the governmental organisations, but as it wasn't with Natural England, I was a bit taken aback, accepted his apologies and moved on. Despite this, he followed up with a massive positive, in that he was open to sharing that he has a disability. Once again, it was refreshing that someone leading on EDI is personally representative of an area they're managing professionally. As part of his role, he coordinates their disability staff networks, meaning that he consults with them on any new or changing policies or guidance.

There are 22 staff networks in all, which is a very impressive number, although the Environment Agency does employ more than 12,000 people. Vera Pudilova, who works for the Environment Agency and wrote the reasonable adjustments guidance detailed in Chapter 10, is a co-lead on a specific autism and ADHD network within the Environment Agency with more than 1,000 members. I imagine there won't just be autistic and ADHD employees in the network, because as support mechanisms are reliant on those people who line manage neurodivergent individuals, I expect that they may be members too. It's just as well, as Mikael knows that line managers can often be a barrier to people disclosing a disability, and that they are a focus for training and guidance on neurodivergence. He told me that increasing awareness drives cultural change in EDI, and more line managers are asking for support with their neurodivergent staff. Mikael is passionate about this and is proud of the overall positive shift at the Environment Agency, which he says is shown in the increase in disability declaration rates (not that he was able to divulge the actual data). To be fair, though, no one I spoke to at the Environment Agency said they had any concerns about disclosing their own neurodivergence.

In fact, the feedback I got was overwhelmingly positive, with one person saying that the Environment Agency was way ahead of other organisations when it comes to EDI. This is evident in some of the initiatives Mikael shared with me. It has been working in partnership with other Defra group stakeholders like Natural England, and with organisations such as Tinnitus UK and the Business Disability Forum to access resources for colleagues with disabilities and to try and make the sector more inclusive and accessible. This involves cross-party working, collaboration and best-practice sharing, but also involves the staff networks leading events to increase their outreach and membership. Mikael told me that one of the most powerful aspects of his job is when someone attends an event like this, has a realisation that other people are like them, and can discuss it in this safe space. It has also been overhauling its recruitment practices, beginning with a series of workshops looking at all aspects of the process, from inclusive language in job adverts to putting adjustments in place in advance of interviews. One piece of incredible practice is its use of 'inclusive recruitment volunteers', who can quality assure the recruitment process at any stage, checking for things like prejudice and unconscious bias. Despite the changes to how the Environment Agency recruits and selects, Mikael was clear that there's still a lot of work to do.

He then casually dropped in a mention of the 'respect at work' network and advisers, and all I could say was 'wow.' Basically, voluntary advisers have undertaken specific training so that colleagues who have a grievance can approach them and discuss it in a safe forum. They are then able to signpost different avenues of support depending on the circumstance. In essence, the advisers are often supporting people to overcome barriers. This led us neatly into speaking about adjustments, and Mikael said something interesting, that the organisation has found upwards of 90 per cent of adjustments easy to implement, with many being accommodations around commitments and scheduling. I spoke to lots of employees at the Environment Agency who all had a range of measures in place to support them at work. Some are practical, like an ergonomic mouse (for dyspraxia), standing desks and noise-cancelling headphones, while others are things that have become more common since the Covid pandemic. Working flexibly and from home also underpins the Environment Agency's commitments to inclusion and valuing everyone, which is why it was an option available to almost everyone who came forward. It uses the industry-standard passport system, and while this was originally just for people identifying with a protected characteristic, it is now rolling them out for everyone in the organisation, which is a sign of an inclusive culture.

We paused, and Mikael stepped back to reflect on our conversation. He said that the last 20 to 30 years had been quite static within the EDI sphere, but there was an inflection point with the murder of George Floyd in 2020, leading to an increase in work on race, diversity and organisational culture in all sectors. This momentum for EDI then bled into other protected characteristics, such as disability, and he feels proud of the people who set the early wheels in motion for EDI work, enabling professionals like him to develop resilient and future-proof processes. He continues to develop these, his current aim being to acquire Level-3 Disability Confident accreditation. He feels the Environment Agency works in a positive way, using the grassroots approach with staff networks, and then ensuring there's representation from senior leadership, who can lend their voice to important and relevant causes. To me, that's an inclusive culture in action, from the bottom to the top and back down again. Mikael added that the chief executive actively engages with the staff networks, fielding difficult questions, and sometimes speaking to staff on an individual basis. This visible leadership is a vital component of driving that inclusive culture forward.

The Forestry Commission is the final body within Defra that I spoke to, specifically its diversity and well-being manager, Wali Rahman. Wali sits in the organisational development team and is British Asian, demonstrating representation in action again. The Commission is made up of three divisions: Forestry England, who manage its woodland sites; Forest Research, its forestry and tree scientists; and Forest Services, who are the government's expert forestry advisers. In all, they employ well over 2,000 staff, and as well as being a part of the civil service, generate additional income from commercial activities, such as car-parking. The Forestry Commission's Diversity and Inclusion Strategy guides its work and brings together its mission to make the Forestry Commission inclusive to all. Its most recent EDI data shows a 7 per cent declaration rate for disability, up from 6 per cent in 2023, and 4 per cent in 2019. Its equality monitoring report is a wonderfully inclusive document, with an aesthetic and language that doesn't feel corporate. It features my favourite visual, the infographic, and lots of pictures of staff members delivering and engaging with EDI work. It also outlines the Forestry Commission's four staff networks, with its 'Disability, Neurodivergence and Carers Staff Network' being the most relevant here.

Wali explained that this network is voluntarily led by staff, mainly two co-chairs, with roughly 100 members and representation from a senior level. Wali's team and the network collaborate in several ways, including the facilitation of events and training. These are external, too, as Wali champions widening the participation in EDI events with the wider civil service and beyond. Prospective changes are run past the networks to ensure inclusivity, and the networks also produce guidance for all staff, such as a recent 'toolkit for neuroinclusive meetings', which was put together by one of the co-chairs. There is also an inclusive workplace practices working group, which is putting together guidance on how to make workspaces and events inclusive for all, including neurodivergent colleagues and stakeholders. Other initiatives I've read about are Inclusion Ambassadors and the Everyone Belongs board. Wali tells me that there are over 40 inclusion ambassadors in place, all of whom have had training to promote and champion diversity and inclusion within their own teams. The Everyone Belongs board provides oversight, assurance and coordination of the Forestry Commission's programmes of work relating to EDI. The Disability, Neurodivergence and Carers Staff Network's steering group has senior representatives from across the organisation and its divisions, who champion the inclusive culture of the organisation.

Another collaborative area is the use of workplace adjustment passports, which the network helps to promote to the wider organisation. Although the long-term aim is for HR to lead on this, Wali shared some of the adjustments in the central team he works in, such as recently setting up a quiet space in their central offices. It has multiple uses – somewhere to meditate, to use for prayer, and, as I suggested, a brilliant place for neurodivergent people to use for self-regulation. I spoke to a member of staff who currently works for Forestry England and they described the organisation as taking reasonable adjustments seriously. Discussions about their own adjustments were timely, extensive and ready to roll from their first day of employment. They praised the overall inclusive culture of the organisation and how it cascades down, especially through line management, which is an area of definite strength for the Forestry Commission when it comes to supporting neurodivergent staff members. This encourages everyone to love the culture themselves, which is the overall aim. They basically validated everything Wali and I had spoken about. It was so fantastic to hear this and to feel the culture in the words of staff across the organisation.

I was way off the mark with my initial belief that the governmental organisations wouldn't want to participate in this book. Not only did they openly discuss their work with me, but overall, I felt like they all demonstrated a genuine commitment to EDI. It was empowering to discover that although these organisations all sit under the umbrella of Defra and adhere to its strategic actions and processes, they all retain their own identity when it comes to EDI work. Each of them employs people to work specifically on this, and there is representation from a diverse range of people. The general rhetoric speaks of striving towards an inclusive culture, and I don't feel like anyone gave me what I would call 'EDI lip service.' Alongside policies, plans and processes, I've been shown material examples of actions being taken, and perhaps most powerfully, no one took to hiding any shortcomings, instead choosing to be honest about their areas for improvement. I wasn't expecting this and thought I'd be met with resistance or even silence in deference to a higher power, but there was no suppression at all. I was reminded that, as with neurodivergence, we should never make assumptions because of our own experiences.

CHAPTER TWELVE
I think I'll eat my lunch in the bat chat corner today

Smaller conservation charities

Alongside all the larger NGOs and governmental organisations, the conservation sector includes many smaller charities and organisations striving towards the same goal: to conserve our environment. In the early days of researching this book, I reached out to every UK nature organisation I could find. Around half responded, and of those, roughly half provided insights significant enough to include. As the number of contributors grew, I followed up with several organisations, and in the end, many offered something tangible and useable.

If a smaller organisation is missing from this chapter, it may be because they didn't respond, chose not to participate, or weren't in a position to share anything at the time. However, I want to be clear: the NGOs and governmental organisations discussed in the last two chapters have access to vastly greater funding and resources. I recognise that smaller organisations often face significant barriers, and I deeply appreciate everyone that took the time to contribute – especially those working without the backing of large corporate frameworks or budgets.

This was illustrated when I got in touch with the British Dragonfly Society through its engagement officer, Lauren Kennedy. Her response was apologetic in tone, sharing that as it's such a small charity, with only six members of staff, it simply doesn't have the structures I was exploring. What this does mean though is that those staff are able to be flexible in how they work, and they adjust for each other, if the need arises, in an informal and reflective way. Lauren noted that they're more like a family in this respect. This is driven by their positive approach to team communication. They all work remotely from home and meet online at least once a month, with a lot of informal communication in between. They also have staff away-day trips once a year, which help them to get to know each other better, thus enhancing their ability to support one another. Lauren was keen to add that they work closely with their trustee board, which allows staff to input into direction and strategy, something that can be difficult to achieve in larger organisations. A recent change has seen them appoint a trustee to specifically focus on EDI to inform policy and structure as the organisation grows, ensuring it remains current.

What I particularly like about these smaller organisations is their specificity. With the three large NGOs from Chapter 10, what you see are the lynchpins of the UK conservation sector. Long-standing household names who serve a general purpose, whether that's wildlife, birds, habitat or heritage. Smaller conservation organisations tend to focus on areas that are more niche. They're more likely to home in on an explicit species or classification. There are people conserving anything from wildflowers and mammals to bats and butterflies. It almost feels like a subculture under the umbrella of NGOs and governmental organisations, and I love it, especially the connotations with neurodivergence. By this I mean that someone is much more likely to have a hyperfocus or special interest in a microcosmic aspect of nomenclature, rather than just nature in general. That much is evident from the people I've spoken to for this book. What better place to start than the workplace of Hazel Jackson? You may recall that

Hazel is the head of conservation outcomes and evidence at the Woodland Trust.

The Woodland Trust isn't exactly a small charity, employing more than 550 people, but in terms of comparative size to the three main conservation NGOs, it's 'small'. On its website, it describes itself as 'the UK's largest woodland conservation charity', with a vision for 'a world where woods and trees thrive for people and nature.' I also like the four simple headings for its work: it protects, restores, creates and cares (for) woodlands. The trust was founded in 1972 by Kenneth Watkins, who had been a farmer and agricultural machinery producer. He and some friends had collective concerns about the decline of the UK's woodlands and bought a small one to try and mitigate this. Over the next 5 years, they took ownership of 22 woodlands in 6 south-western counties. Today, the Trust is responsible for more than 1,000 woodlands nationwide. The Trust is expressly clear that its organisation isn't diverse enough and doesn't reflect UK society. I respect and applaud it for sharing this so openly and prominently. I chatted to a staff member about EDI, and as I anticipated, the Trust collects disability data, just not on neurodivergence. It approximates that 10 per cent of its staff identify as having a disability.

As with most organisations, it utilises an internal intranet for this, where stories from neurodivergent staff are shared. Signposting is provided to sources of support, such as guidance and webinars for managers, and a well-being action plan for individuals to define the things that will help them thrive at work. The latter is, in all but name, a workplace passport system. Hazel told me about the Woodland Trust's online platform, 'the Treehouse', which is a social space for all staff. Within this are various channels, including an inclusion book club, and a specific network for disability and neurodiversity. The platform is private, to ensure that it's a safe space for those who choose to access it. The network is actively run by volunteers who endeavour to facilitate conversation at all levels. Hazel believes that uniting all these strands in one place is imperative for ensuring that all staff are aware of what they can access. She also told me about the Trust's online training platform, 'Roots', which hosts a neurodiversity module made by the Trust. They put out a launch video for this, where two senior leaders spoke about their own experiences of being neurodivergent, sharing their journeys, their feelings about neurodiversity, and their desire to empower others.

Of course, Hazel was one of the leaders, and shared that the feedback on this was resoundingly positive, especially on how powerful it was to have two senior staff speaking openly about their own neurodivergence. She added that after the launch, several people got in touch with her directly to thank her, and to share how much more comfortable they now feel about discussing it, addressing it, and asking for support. The power of senior leaders sharing their own experiences of neurodivergence couldn't be more clear than in these words. I found more evidence in the Woodland Trust's most recent annual report. Firstly, in its strategic aims up to 2030, under the title 'Transform', stating that it's 'transforming how we operate, ensuring we are the high-performing, inclusive team our cause needs us to be.' It also outlines its work to widen participation, with a focus on engaging younger people. This led to the creation of the 'Youth Reimagined' programme, listing its key achievements as setting up a youth panel, creating two temporary jobs and multiple placements for young people, and appointing one trustee under 30. As a final note, Hazel shared this section of the book with a director to check, and guess what, they happen to be neurodivergent, too.

I also heard back from Plantlife International, a small charity of just under 60 employees, whose aim is 'to protect and restore a wide variety of wild plants and fungi in our countryside, towns and cities.' It works across a diverse range of habitats with the goal of ensuring that the UK's most common species of plants aren't under threat. Plantlife's media and campaigns manager provided me with a lovely little summary of its EDI work, saying that the charity has an active EDI committee that meets monthly, is open to all staff, and has director-level representation, including a board-level EDI lead. Plantlife recently undertook a staff survey to capture diversity data, and of the 70 per cent of staff completing the survey, 10 per cent specifically identify as neurodivergent. I make that to be four staff members. Plantlife also actively participates in wider information sharing and good practice networks in the EDI arena, to better inform its own work. This recently led to the introduction of collecting anonymous EDI data at the recruitment stage. Finally, Plantlife incorporates training around neurodivergence, with the ADHD Foundation recently presenting to it on 'Celebrating Neurodiversity in the Workplace'.

Another charity that was keen to contribute was the Mammal Society. It may be small, employing only six people, but its chief executive, Matt Larsen-Daw, didn't shy away from my questions. Founded in 1954, its overarching aim is for 'a 'future in which sustainable mammal populations thrive as part of healthy and diverse ecosystems.' It is proudly science-led, and lists 34 local mammal groups that feed into its national oversight. Matt told me that out of six staff, one self-identifies as neurodivergent, but as they're such a compact team, they're able to flex their plans and working practices around the ideal conditions of all staff. They recognise that everyone is different and that they must all work together to facilitate genuine inclusion. Something they did, as a 'soft' introduction to the different ways people work, was to get all team members to complete some personality tests and then discuss the results together at an away day. One of the tests gives you an animal representation of your personality, an owl for example, and although genial, approaches such as this help to normalise discussions around differences.

The Mammal Society doesn't have a passport system, and in all fairness, with such a small number of staff, there probably isn't the need. Matt told me that all staff have a Personal Development Plan, made in conjunction with their line manager, and as part of this they'll reflect on any needs or challenges they may wish to work on, to build confidence within and beyond the workplace. I asked about any specific adjustments, and he shared an example that typifies neuroinclusive culture. If someone doesn't attend a meeting, or does so with their video off, there's a mutual understanding that it'll be for a good reason and there's no need for an explanation. This is part of their 'prioritise yourself' culture, an important element of their team dynamic, leading to better communication and ultimately, better results in collaborative projects. Matt is incredibly passionate about this and went on to describe how rigid expectations and structures often force people to plough through anxiety and overwhelm, when what they need is some time and space to reflect. He also spoke about the education system from a position of personal and professional experience, and how it can get things so right but also woefully wrong.

Matt believes that anyone can reach their maximum potential and contribute as best as they are able to when processes and activities don't force them to participate in conditions that are ideal for some but inappropriate and damaging for others. We both agreed that this should apply in all areas of life, and that people who manage others can embed this into their workplace so that everyone reaps the benefits. Matt takes a holistic view of supporting individual differences, too. He noted that while the increase in understanding about neurodivergence can bring numerous positive benefits, a truly inclusive workplace allows everyone to be their unique self, which may not fit any neat label. He believes that in this context, those who wouldn't self-identify as neurodivergent, or don't have a formal diagnosis, are still able to benefit from the same approaches and adjustments, which also means that no accommodation is seen as accommodating just one individual's needs. It's no surprise that Matt and the Mammal Society are, in his words, looking at creating education resources and activities that utilise the unique benefits of studying and interacting with nature to nurture neurodivergent young people's talents and interests.

I asked if the Mammal Society have any other initiatives Matt would like to share with me, which he did. He's proud that it's an inclusive employer, and expressly invites candidates with additional requirements to apply for their roles. Its inclusive recruitment practices are evident in all job adverts and on its website. Matt explained that this can help to reduce anxiety and encourage people to join the organisation, who might otherwise believe they'll find themselves in an unwelcoming or harmful environment. The Mammal

Society's job adverts also explain the recruitment process, to help candidates envisage what might happen before they apply. At interview stage, interviewers are explicit that candidates can pause or take time out as and when they may need to. This includes turning the video off in an online interview, all without penalisation. Inclusive recruitment is something that's gaining momentum in the EDI sphere, and it was helpful that Matt set out what his organisation are doing regarding this, because in such a small setting, it's likely they'll be doing this all themselves. Their next steps are to devolve more inclusive practice to their local groups network, through further training and resource development. Matt and the Mammal Society truly breathe inclusivity.

I also had a brief discussion with the chief executive of the Bumblebee Conservation Trust, Gill Perkins. I didn't know much about this organisation, so I had a look, and its website says that the Trust has been around since 2006, and was set up by Professor Dave Goulson, who is a leading insect and bumblebee conservationist and author of vital books like *Silent Earth*. The charity's vision is for a 'world where bumblebees are thriving and valued by everyone.' Employing more than 60 people, it uses science and research to guide and inform policy, as well as work on conserving and creating habitats for bees. Gill told me that they take EDI very seriously, and obviously this includes neurodiversity. In 2023, they brought in a series of neurodiversity awareness workshops from consultant Matt Gupwell. Gill reported that these were excellent and shared the post-session slides with me, which were insightful and engaging. Afterwards, they held an online feedback session for all staff to discuss their reactions and what they took away from it. Gill thinks everyone naturally makes adjustments, but on a personal level she feels much more aware of how we're all different, and now makes some specific adjustments for those people she works with closely.

On the Bumblebee Conservation Trust website is an EDI statement which outlines its commitments to making the trust more equitable, diverse and inclusive. It covers the things I've come to expect now, such as barriers, culture and valuing differences. Gill told me that the website is new and in due course will feature much more, but she sent me the EDI policy directly and it's a solid document. She couldn't share any statistics with me but made a lovely point that it isn't about data, it's about evaluating whether there's a genuine increase in awareness of neurodiversity. Since their awareness training, the Trust's recruitment team have put their own mandatory neurodiversity training into their induction process, which is becoming much more commonplace now. They also include a recording of Matt's training as part of this, which I view as a particularly accessible addition. Alongside this, they've set up an EDI working group, which is open to all Trust staff and feeds directly into future organisational planning, where they aim to weave EDI into everything they do, such as recruitment processes and project management. I have the utmost respect for any organisation that acknowledges it's on a journey with this.

Regarding small flying things with six legs, I also spoke to the EDI lead at the national charity Butterfly Conservation. Over the years, I've been an on-and-off member of this organisation, and I'm a fan of their work. At the start of the book, I said how much I love moths, and since they sit in the same taxonomic order as butterflies, Lepidoptera, I'm partial to a butterfly as well. Butterfly Conservation employs just over 90 people, and sets its aim out as wanting 'to see a world where butterflies and moths thrive and can be enjoyed by everyone, forever.' The EDI lead at Butterfly Conservation (at the time) was one of the first people at an organisation to reply to me. They were forthcoming, sharing some basic information long before I'd begun to hone the specifics of what I was looking to find out about EDI and neurodivergence across the sector. First, as always, I had a look at their 'visible EDI'. It felt like a bit of a goldmine and there was a lot of information they were keen to share with me about their work.

The EDI lead said that, as an organisation, Butterfly Conservation aims to promote diversity and inclusion in everything it does, such as moving towards inclusive competency and values-driven recruitment processes, and using outreach and project work to engage diverse communities. The HR team have begun a programme to update their EDI work, starting with their statement of intent. Back when I first spoke to them, their annual staff survey had given the figure of 20 per cent of staff members identifying as having a long-term physical or mental health condition. In a more recent news article, Butterfly Conservation refer to making progress with their EDI work and confirmed an increase to 22 per cent in their declaration data. I look forward to reading more updates from them.

Another organisation to respond to me was the British Trust for Ornithology (BTO). The BTO is a non-governmental, non-campaigning organisation that focuses on 'securing the future for birds and nature.' It describes the heart of its organisation as encompassing three key areas: birds, science and people. Regarding the last, I spoke to some current and former staff, who said that the overarching narrative of the BTO and neurodivergence is complex, and after some difficult times is moving in a positive direction. One employee described the BTO as being on a 'neurodivergence journey', and that the culture toward neurodivergence was both inclusive and supportive. However, they felt that actual practices weren't always fully inclusive, and that this led to considerable stress and anxiety for some neurodivergent staff, who felt their concerns weren't being taken seriously, with a few choosing to leave. It's worth remembering, though, that there are two sides to every story. The employee said that the turning point was when the BTO began to go through a process of realisation that it was lacking in this area, leading to a raft of changes in organisational practice and culture that this employee was all too happy to share with me.

A neurodiversity working group was set up to provide a voice for these staff and advocate for them. The employee feels like there's been a cultural shift, with an increase in acceptance and awareness at all levels of the organisation, as well as adjustments and Access to Work recommendations now being put in place swiftly and effectively. The employee described the BTO as continuing to work hard to improve in this area, which is wonderful to hear and to be able to write. Several staff were clear that upon changing their line managers, their experience suddenly became positive, even transformative. I suppose that every person in employment is playing a 'line-management lottery'. A culture can always shift, but a few difficult staff can make this process take a lot longer than it perhaps needs to. All the staff that I spoke to were keen to share that the adjustments they need are now in place, and all of them feel their line managers have a much better understanding of their conditions and how to adjust for them than they did before. As I said, change can sometimes take time.

From birds to bats, and the work of the Bat Conservation Trust (BCT), a small charity employing just under 40 people. As you might expect, its focus is on bats, and its vision is of 'a world rich in wildlife where bats and people thrive together.' Its website states that it is the largest UK NGO solely focusing on the conservation of bats and their habitats. I spoke to their director of communications and fundraising, Joe Nunez-Mino, who said that they're proud of their efforts to make their work more inclusive and welcoming to a more diverse range of people. He outlines their commitment to inclusion in their governing document, which states that as an organisation the BCT will 'act with due regard to our commitment to championing Equity, Diversity and Inclusion throughout all of our work and to act in accordance with the Charity's EDI Statement of Values.' The latter is something that Joe shared with me, and it is also available online. It's what I hope to see in an EDI statement, but I particularly like the references to the link between biodiversity and diversity, and the fact they invite feedback on their EDI work as they continually develop it.

A quote that particularly stood out to me is that the BCT 'recognise there can be many barriers to connecting with nature and engaging with conservation and that systemic issues and systems of oppression impact different groups in different ways.' However, the organisation has faced backlash for addressing these issues – most notably when it supported a submission from Wildlife and Countryside Link to an All-Party Parliamentary Group examining racism and the environmental emergency. Some portions of the mainstream media misrepresented the document, suggesting it labelled the countryside as a 'racist and colonial space', despite all signatories making clear that it referenced historical events, legacies and lived experiences.

Unsurprisingly, this led to negative press coverage, with some outlets portraying BCT and other conservationists as overly sensitive. One particularly bizarre article seemed intent on discrediting the Trust but ultimately did little more than present facts with quotation marks around them. The reader comments were even worse – discriminatory, unfounded and needlessly hostile. It's disheartening to see solidarity and allyship so often weaponised against those advocating for inclusivity, especially when organisations like the BCT are actively working to make their spaces more welcoming.

One of my favourite examples of this is their approach to event accessibility. Joe shared with me that the BCT designate specific areas for people who wish to mingle in breaks and are introducing what they call a 'Bat Chat Corner', which I think is a great idea. A space where individuals or small groups can sit to indicate they would welcome the opportunity to chat with others.

Back to the organisation as a workplace. A simple but effective adjustment it has put in place is to adjust the slide template for its staff away day to make it easier for neurodivergent people to read. This was successful, and it is now incorporating it into new BCT brand guidelines, which are currently in development. Almost all the organisations I've spoken to have an internal staff network for EDI and the BCT is no exception. Its EDI channel is open to all staff for sharing experiences, best practice/knowledge and resources. The Trust is also proud to have an active EDI working group, who meet regularly to further develop their EDI work. Obviously, I was going to ask Joe about senior representation in this group, but he had already included this in his response. Yes, there are representatives from the board of trustees, the senior management team and all departments in the organisation. Joe went in strongly, saying that they're proud of what they've been doing around inclusive practice, and they should be, but I don't think he'd mind me saying that there will always be more work to do on EDI, and this applies to everyone I've spoken to.

That said, what I find most refreshing about the BCT is that they acknowledge this, and openly ask for feedback and ideas. I spoke to their chief executive, Kit Stoner, to ask if she could share a few words on EDI, and she said that the culture at the BCT is one of inclusivity. They recognise the strength of having diversity amongst their staff, including neurodiversity, and aim to provide any support they may need. Kit loves that neurodiverse staff at BCT have felt comfortable enough to give the organisation feedback on where they're doing well, but also on where they can improve. This learning has been important in guiding them on the journey to extending that support further, to volunteers and others that they work with.

Throughout my investigation into EDI at smaller conservation charities, it has been great to find a set of professionals and organisations willing to put their heads above the proverbial parapet and underline their genuine commitment to EDI and neurodivergence, but also to transparency and integrity. What I've found particularly powerful is that despite sometimes only having a handful of staff, these smaller organisations still put everything in place for neuroinclusion, from an employment law perspective, but also just as decent people and employers.

Ultimately, if you make your organisation the best place to work that you can, then what you get is happy and productive staff able to dedicate themselves to a cause. Anyone can thrive in a supportive environment that adapts to meet their needs, and this can have a knock-on positive effect on people who manage others, as the potential for people having to take sick days due to unmet needs can lessen, for example.

There are many details I've chosen not to put in the book. I've written about this already and could say much more, but dwelling on frustration wouldn't be productive and risks causing unnecessary harm. I also choose not to name or criticise the organisations that declined to participate or didn't engage as fully as others. My goal was to offer every organisation I contacted a platform to share and celebrate their EDI work, particularly around neurodiversity. The fact that not everyone took up that opportunity is a reminder that there's still progress to be made before EDI becomes central to everything we do. As I write, I ebb and flow between accepting that this is the current reality and feeling frustrated at the persistent gaps in inclusivity that I've witnessed. But I'm hopeful that if we keep pushing forward, our voices will only grow stronger.

In one exchange, a senior staff member of an organisation in the conservation sector said that they felt the main takeaway from our discussions was this: If a whole organisation is going to create a culture that's truly neuroinclusive and be a place where all neuro-types can thrive, support needs to come right from the top and in a timely manner. The biggest challenge this person says they face is in convincing senior leadership about the benefits of actively promoting and supporting neurodiversity. This is the perfect fork in the road to head down one of the final pathways of the book. We need to rewind the clock and go back to where I believe we can make the biggest difference to conserving our future. It's time to focus on the younger generation and consider what we can do to plant the proverbial seeds of interest, which might grow and flourish, to bloom into the conservationists of tomorrow (and all that metaphorical jazz).

CHAPTER THIRTEEN

Just give the naughtiest ones a sprig of lavender and a circular saw

Forest schools and care farms

For neurodivergent people to unearth the intrinsic connection with nature that they seem to have, they must be given the opportunities to put down their metaphorical roots. Of course, the earlier we give people this opportunity, the more chance we have of creating a legacy of interest in the outdoors and its benefits. Therefore, we must begin nurturing this during childhood and throughout education, whether formally or informally. As I've already said, our current results-driven system isn't built to promote outdoor learning and genuine nature connection. Due to the focus on exam results and outcomes, these approaches seem even less prevalent in the secondary education phase and often appear to be the preserve of the private institution or those offering alternative frameworks of learning. However, many schools provide outdoor activities via their extracurricular or enrichment programmes, which do at least give those with an interest the chance to develop it further. Many also facilitate their own eco clubs or councils, which are often led by young people and can lead to national recognition and accreditation for those able to prove their eco credentials.

By 'alternative frameworks of learning', I was primarily alluding to what are known in education circles as 'alternative provisions', or APs. The use of these is becoming increasingly common, as more people recognise that the mainstream model doesn't always work for neurodivergent children. APs are bespoke provisions that cater for individual needs by offering approaches and activities that are designed to engage certain young people much more positively than traditional approaches. Throughout my own career, I've been commissioning and using APs to supplement and enhance the mainstream educational packages of children with SEND, many of whom have not had a positive experience of school. These placements almost always lead to improvements in wellbeing, engagement and attendance, and often help with pathway planning, particularly for those who go to an AP with a vocational offer. For example, attending an AP that delivers construction skills (possibly with accreditation), could not only ignite an interest in this area of trade, but also generate the desire to work towards a related career. However, the vast majority of APs I've put in place for the young people I work with have had a focus on outdoor experiences and nature connection.

This doesn't mean I've deliberately made all the children that I work with go to an outdoor AP because I love nature. Negotiating, discussing and visiting these provisions prior to commissioning them is something that I've always done with young people and those with parental responsibility for them. It is good practice, and it ensures that young people and their carers are at the heart of any decision-making. It just so happens that many of them have leant towards wanting to be outdoors, which as they've all been neurodivergent, must be more than just a coincidence, right? The most obvious approach, and one you're most likely to recognise, is forest school. Forest school is a pedagogic construct focusing on personal growth through social constructs, play and exploration in (mostly) woodland settings. It centres on experiential learning, encourages risk-taking, and is shown to develop confidence and self-esteem through hands-on outdoor experiences. Its roots go back to the nineteenth century, but it is widely thought to have arisen in the UK from a group of Somerset nursery nurses visiting preschools in Denmark during 1993. After seeing the Scandinavian approach to outdoor play and learning, they came back and set up their own 'forest school'. The rest, as they say, is history.

It took me a while to find the right forest school to fit with the book and with my own perspectives on outdoor education. In the end, it couldn't have fallen into place any more perfectly, as the ethos and approach of the one I chose were so congruent with my own, it felt like a match made in heaven. The Wilderness Grove is a family-run forest school, set in over three acres of mature woodland near Cringleford, south Norfolk, within a county wildlife site called Intwood Carr. Their website states that their sessions 'provide a safe, secure way for children to explore nature and the way they learn.' They describe giving people real freedom to do this, and as well as outlining the instructional activities they offer, they are explicit that anyone who attends can just go there and enjoy the surroundings. As one of the main barriers to accessing mainstream education is the pressure of expectation, the fact that the Grove is open to removing this entirely is wonderfully refreshing. It's run by couple Cate Regi and Tom Wild, who bought the woodland plot in May 2020 and opened the Grove in the September.

Having had Cate engage positively with me when I contacted the school, I can't wait to meet her on the day I visit. When I pull up though, I have a bit of an anxiety attack, feeling like everyone is staring at me, and almost freak out and bail. Thankfully Cate appears, spies my confusion, and takes me up to a seating area next to a hut to recalibrate and have a chat. Her background is in education and isn't too dissimilar to my own. She has spent time working across a plethora of settings, including pupil referral units, specialist, mainstream and secure units. She's an art teacher, but has taught across all the phases and to adults as well, saying that she's taught from 'nought to ninety-six'. She has always leant towards people with SEND, much like I have, and I can feel the authenticity and empathy oozing from her as she speaks about her career. When they bought the site, it was horrendously overgrown, derelict and damp, as it sits across three flood zones. They spent their days there clearing and building, and the nights wild camping. She shows me the area that was their initial focus, and the fire pit and den that they built in those early days.

As a family, they're woven into the history and fabric of the site, which you can feel in the way that Cate describes it. We pass a tyre swing, which is a popular location for people to self-regulate, and step down into the stream that runs along the northern boundary. The water is so clear as it trickles around our wellies; its banks swell with young green reeds, herb robert, and red campion. I'm loving the scenic route. We stop, and Cate explains how the stream often needs to be dug out to drain excess water away. This can present learning opportunities in the most surprising of ways, from what Cate describes as 'slugs and foxgloves, to iron deposits'. I love the elemental way in which they're able to teach and impart learning; it's intrinsic and beautiful. We pop up the bank to the 'kitchen', where Cate shows me their Nordic fridge, which is essentially a giant cool box. I ask where the food comes from, and she explains that they receive food from the charity RE:Think, who repurpose waste food in Norfolk, and the Grove does a bi-weekly pick-up. This enables their young people to explore and play with the food, which can be beneficial for those with restrictive eating habits.

All around me are examples of where activities are set up for anyone to access, but with no expectation that they will be used, such as a plastic table with lipped edges, on top of which sit bowls of dried leaves, a floury batter, and some lavender. These are purely for exploration, mainly from a sensory perspective. It's simple but enticing, and I run my hands through the lavender, inhaling the floral aroma. There's another table next to it, with seats made from tree stumps between them, this one has a freeform art activity using twigs, clay, wood offcuts and wood shavings. She shows me a creepy death mask-type creation, which I quite admire. Deeper into the site are ponds, sculptures, arches and dens, all woven from natural materials, mainly willow. I ask Cate if they run any specific groups for neurodivergent children, which they don't. However, she believes their cohort, which is made up of young people attending AP and those from home-education, is easily 99 per cent neurodivergent. All groupings are put together collaboratively by looking at the peer dynamics, and a lot of thought goes into this. For example, they wouldn't place a child who struggles with sensory processing in a group that may be over-stimulating.

I ask how they measure and share progress with commissioning schools and parents and carers. Cate shows me the app they use for this, which is an online early-years platform. We discuss how much more holistic and organic the early-years curriculum is and how this translates perfectly into an outdoor AP. The app enables the team to map each individual learning journey, using photos and narration, and holds contact and general information. Any posts automatically share with the person commissioning the AP, acting as evidence and a communication tool. I like it. What sort of outcomes are they measuring and working towards? The beauty of how the site is set up means that young people can engage with whatever they are drawn to. Ultimately, when a young person is drawn to a particular area or activity, the reasons behind this are interesting, too. What this means is that the team works dynamically and are constantly looking out for learning opportunities. I ask if this means that there's no formal planning, expecting there not to be anything in place. However, Cate, with her education hat on, shows me some examples of their overviews, which are rich in detail and differentiation. It's very impressive.

Two of the main areas that referrers ask Wilderness Grove to work on are social skills and self-regulation. They approach this through ensuring that all their activities focus on developing a greater sense of self. This spills out into a flowchart of sorts; from focusing on the self, it moves on to peers, and the team will then look to add other young people into the mix, for collaboration and communication. This is the foundation for the next step, which is to develop these skills further in the safe environment of the Grove, before taking them outside and using them in wider social situations. We're standing in Tom's domain now; half of a large open barn structure, with workbenches along one side, and a forge, where he repurposes metal tools for a hobby. He shows me various axes he's given a new lease of life to, including one that a young person brought in which was their grandad's. Not only are they stunning and lovingly done, but the emotional connection of this example is a powerful thing. Then he lets me have a go at a treadle wheel, which is basically a pedal-driven band saw. Naturally, I can't do it, and Tom shows me how.

I love how something as simple as the treadle can support so many areas of need, from proprioception (body awareness) to hand-eye coordination. Tom says that this is what his approach is all about, and I reflect that although my focus has always been on the nature connection side of outdoor learning, practical tasks provide so many benefits too. Standing in the pole barn, I realise how much I like it in there. It's reflective of Cate and Tom, with his workshop on one side of a partition, and Cate's creative space on the other. It's homely on her side; a dining table and chairs sit on a rug in front of a woodburner. Along the partition wall is a line of tray units, like those you might find in a traditional primary school classroom, each containing different art materials, with labels to encourage exploration. We stand and chat for a while. Tom shows me more of the tools he has brought back from the brink, and Cate gets out some giant sketch books containing artwork by both her and the young people who attend the Grove. A lot of this is stunning stuff. Vibrant, abstract and elemental, and all made in a safe but communal way.

There's even more to see. Cate takes me further into the woodland, where extensive 'mud kitchens' are hidden, along with play areas that the young people have made themselves. Away from the safer spaces of the pole barn and the kitchen, it feels wider and more exploratory. Here is where the compost toilet resides, as well as a yurt for the older children to spend time in. Even as the rain drips down heavily through the trees, I'm drawn to one of the climbing areas and the colourful pennants along the top of it. Cate says that this has been a focus this term, and young people have been not only decorating this treehouse area but also adding pulleys and nets to help them overcome obstacles.

What I really like about Cate and Tom is that they're a bit yin and yang, but that's what makes them so effective. Cate's career path is in art and education, and Tom's background is in farming. Cate focuses on the strategic and operational, whereas Tom is more hands-on and 'likes to chop wood and lug stuff', but there's so much more to him than that. I ask them both what it is about their provision that works for neurodivergence. Cate says that behaviours that seem inappropriate for the classroom usually manifest because of control, whether a lack of it, or too much. When you're outside, you must relinquish that control to nature. Tom adds that the 'naughty kid in the classroom becomes a leader outdoors,' which I love. They say that forest school is a low-demand approach, removing the fear of failure that often comes with mainstream school. This reminds me of the concept of natural environments being non-judgemental. Cate says that being outdoors has interoceptive qualities, which basically means that it helps people to feel internal sensations in their body, from their breathing to their emotions. In this sense, Tom says, being outside is innate.

Another approach seen in outdoor APs is the concept of 'care farming'. Some years ago, I set up a placement at a care farm for one of the students I was working with. I went along a few times during a settling period, and I was completely blown away by what I saw and some of the chats I had with the owners. A care farm is a farm that uses farming practices therapeutically. They were overseen by Care Farming UK until a merger with the Federation of City Farms and Community Gardens in 2018 formed a new organisation, Social Farms and Gardens. Care farms, sometimes known as social farms, must have structure, be able to supervise as well as support, and provide this on a regular basis, not just as a one-off intervention. Similarly to forest schools, they embed social communication, teamwork and problem-solving, as well as the learning of specific skills relative to the farm itself. Most are working farms in some capacity, and this offers a unique opportunity for young people to help run farms when they are there.

Many care farms keep animals, which are proven to have therapeutic benefits in such contexts. Alex Harding, the outdoor learning coordinator, works with several of his local farms, on both a short- and long-term basis, and heaps praise on the benefit of any provision that provides contact and interaction with animals. He says that working closely with animals tunes into non-verbal communication. He observes that a quiet young person can sit stroking a rabbit and just be in the moment, or they can lead a horse without speaking, but they take notice of the horse's behaviour and respond to it. In an educational context and as an AP, a care farm can provide a different environment for sensory- or emotional-regulation difficulties, being somewhere that's calm and non-judgemental. Many also offer accreditation, to offer finite outcomes as well as developing soft skills. The farm I contacted was Edfords Care Farm, in Mautby, Norfolk, and is run by farmers Chris Howes and Lou Bishop-Howes. They took on the farm in 2019 but had run a care farm for five years prior to this. Edfords spans 84 acres, and hosts pigs, sheep, alpacas, turkeys, chickens, geese and sheepdogs. It's a very special place.

Over a typical week, they work with 60 students, aged 11 to 16, with most being on a school roll, although referring schools do vary, and they also work with several children who are stuck in educational limbo due to an absence of suitable placements for them. Groups are no larger than 16, and Chris suggests that almost all attendees are neurodivergent. They employ 12 paid staff, who may work one-to-one, or even at higher ratios, depending on need. They prefer to use their own support staff for consistency, and to match their ethos and approaches. Finding the right staff for Edfords isn't easy; Chris says you can work with people, work with animals, and work in farming, but rarely can you triangulate the three. A case in point is in the way he and Lou run the farm. Lou is out with the groups, whereas Chris will often be found in the butchery. Activities vary day to day. The first time I visit, there's a whiteboard outlining the tasks that need completing that day. Lou is clear that the list of tasks isn't prescriptive. In an ideal world, they'd all be done, but she and Chris are also realists.

Today, the jobs include feeding the pigs, changing the wires in the electric fences of all the breeding pigs, strawing up the pigs, tidying the market garden (with a sub-checklist of what this entails), clearing the flower garden polytunnel, putting a bale in the front and back of each polytunnel, feeding the alpacas, mucking out the boxes in the barn and mowing the alpaca field. Recalling that when I came all those years ago, Chris was keen to develop accreditation for their work, I suggest using the AQA Unit Award Scheme, a framework I've been successfully using in my own setting, and Lou's face lights up. They have been writing their own units for a while (like I had) and she shows me some, such as 'Setting up an animal enclosure' and 'Preserving rare-breed farm animals'. I ask if they can generalise the tasks undertaken by young people on the farm, which they can. Livestock management, farm conservation (particularly rare breeds) and farm maintenance. They also have their butchery, which is run as a business, preparing pork, lamb and beef to sell to an organic farm shop. They are now, Chris is glad to share, self-sufficient.

There are plans to one day use the butchery in an educational context, but not in the immediate future. Chris shows me around, and it's an impressive new facility, but I can also understand the reasons for keeping it separate. As well as the market garden, across the farm are swathes of meadow where wildflowers are abundant: birds-foot trefoil, scarlet pimpernels and thistles splash colour across the dry earth (it's rather hot on the day I visit). However, Chris says that the students just don't take an interest in horticulture, which is a shame. So, what is it about their approach that works for neurodivergent young people? They treat everyone with equity and respect, because that's the challenge of neurodiversity; everyone's different. Specifics don't always work in this context, so for Chris and Lou it's about the culture they embed and the relationships they build. They say that whilst there are always jobs to be done on the farm, the young people who attend are given the responsibility and individuality to undertake those tasks in the way that works best for them. This is poles apart from the often-regimental structures penning them in at a mainstream school. That's why they're attending Edfords, after all.

A lot of emphasis is put on trust. They have no qualms about a student using a circular saw for a task, whereas their school would probably scream if they saw them with one. As Chris says, it's not the activities that they offer, it's how they offer them that matters. This is where their own backgrounds influence what they do. Chris has always been open with me about his mental health struggles, and Lou has a hearing impairment, so they both understand what it's like to face multiple daily barriers. This is a big part of why they do what they do and invest so much into Edfords. It's beautiful.

I revisit the following week, as I've done the classic ADHD thing of leaving my wellies at the farm and need them, but also because Lou invites me to go and see her Friday group in action. When I arrive, the young people head to the barn to fill up some feed containers and then carry them together, across the farm, to where some of the pigs need moving. Lou and I take the truck and trailer and wait for them to arrive, and they soon do, to start feeding the pigs.

All the young people get stuck in and seem to gravitate towards certain pigs, discussing what needs to be done, and engaging in camaraderie with each other and the staff. They then work together to move the pigs into the trailer. One student is particularly vocal and generally leads on all the tasks. His name is Ethan, and he comes to sit with me at a picnic table whilst I have a coffee. He tells me that school was a negative experience from the start, and attending Edfords has been life-changing for him. I ask why. He says that he can just be himself, take the lead without judgement, and he gets to immerse himself in what he loves. His mum, Emma, says that she fought for 10 months to get him a placement there, as his school just wouldn't accept the potential benefits. He eventually left the school, and the farm became part of his home education package for a day each week. Emma says that within a week he was more confident, less anxious and chattier. People close to them said how different he was, in a positive way.

Now 10 years into the journey of running an AP, Edfords works with over 20 schools and collaborates closely with the local education authority. They sometimes meet with prospective APs to guide and support them, if their ethos aligns with Edfords' own. One thing that Chris and Lou both find incredibly frustrating is the misconception that APs are lacking in structure, which is simply not true, as we learnt from Cate and Tom at Wilderness Grove. It's important to Chris and Lou that everyone who visits the farm understands that it is a working farm, especially the students who attend. Chris doesn't like the term 'care farm'. He thinks it conjures images of a petting zoo, and that the notion of care implies barriers and restrictions. I can't help but agree with him. Edfords is a farm, that's what it is. Why do they continue? Because the most challenging children always have so much more to them than their labels, and at Edfords they appreciate every individual for who they are. The satisfaction of watching them grow, succeed, develop and achieve is what's truly important to Chris and Lou.

There are several other approaches to outdoor learning in the UK, such as bushcraft, adventure activities and orienteering, but I feel that if forest schools and care farms were in place more widely, we'd see huge improvements in the educational experience and well-being of not only neurodivergent young people, but all young people. We also need to look beyond education at other ways to support and inspire the younger generations.

Many years ago, my current career began from working in a variety of youth work roles, and I learnt that direct engagement with young people doesn't just take place in educational settings. Now, with the constant presence of social media, more young people than ever are ready to get involved. In fact, most of the contributors to this book found their way to me via a social media platform, and it's through some of these people that I came across an organisation trailblazing youth engagement in the conservation sector, UK Youth for Nature. Not only am I aware of their social media presence, but I also find that their content comes across as current, accessible and engaging, as does their website, on which they describe themselves as 'the leading UK youth movement calling for urgent action on the nature crisis.'

I contact them and connect with Ellen Bradley, one of their co-directors. She explains to me that UK Youth for Nature, which I'm going to shorten (as they do) to UKY4N from now on, is a UK-wide network of 16–35-year-olds, who specialise in creative campaigning that facilitates discussions between young people and decision makers. She describes the organisation as a mix of people with an interest in conservation, but from hugely diverse backgrounds, including biologists, teachers, artists, theatre set designers, NHS staff and more. This is representation in action, and they celebrate difference, too, through ensuring that everyone has a voice and a role in what they do. They achieve this through utilising the range of skills everyone brings, whether it's art or data management; Ellen is clear that you don't need ecological field skills to be able to contribute to the conservation sector. They're currently focusing on two major campaigns: 'Not so Freshwater', which focuses on the agricultural chemical pollution of our freshwater habitats, and 'Your Wild Streets', which focuses on urban nature and access to it. Ellen is proud of some of the creative campaigning and events that the network has produced so far, and she shares two fantastic examples with me.

The first was when they made a 50m-long sand drawing on Scarborough beach, featuring four biologically significant British species (curlew, oak, salmon and beaver) within the outline of the UK. They began making it in the early morning and by seven o'clock in the evening, the tide had done its work, and it had gone. The message was about declining biodiversity, and it's conveyed in an effective campaign video, which I thoroughly recommend watching on the UKY4N website, if you're able to. The second was an event in London, where they set up a 'chemical cocktail bar' for the attendance of various conservation organisations and parliamentarians. Ellen sent me the recipe cards, which each have eye-catching designs and an accessible layout. Each one represents a major river, such as the 'Tamar-garita', which features the instruction, 'Fill a cocktail shaker with flea treatment, antibiotics, waste from diesel engines, flame retardant and plasticiser, shake thoroughly.' The cards were made in collaboration with the Wildlife and Countryside Link and the Rivers Trust, and they are both aesthetically pleasing and powerful. Ellen is rightfully proud of the success of this event and how they put their message across, and so she should be, as it's utterly brilliant!

Why does Ellen feel that engaging young people with nature is so important? She says we're at a point in tackling the biodiversity crisis where we need innovation, and that's what young people do, they innovate, and their status quo is to challenge the status quo. She adds that although young people can be naive (which is part of being young and learning), that naivety can be a driver and protective factor in the face of something like the climate crisis. She calls it 'useful naivety', as it grounds you in the present, making you less likely to dwell on the enormity of the challenges in front of you and more likely to act. She also feels that the presence of young people can bring a level of emotion into important conversations and decision-making processes that may not usually be there. She says that if you have a young person around the table with you, it adds a different perspective, or 'timestamp', as she calls it, because that young person will live through the changes that you put in place, whereas you might not. I'd never thought about this in such a hard-hitting way before. What she says makes total sense.

I wonder if perhaps the older generation of campaigners and conservationists might feel despondent at fighting a losing battle for so long. They'll have seen many species dying out, habitats disappearing, pollution increasing and green spaces becoming even less accessible, and all of this must take a heavy personal toll when it's your life's work. As Ellen says, young people bring hope, optimism and a youthful exuberance, which can boost the conservation sector during these challenging times. When you throw in all the extras that neurodivergent people can bring, those different perspectives and sharpened senses, you start to see how this all joins up. In neurodivergent young people, there's potentially a huge unspent resource for the conservation sector in plain sight. However, people are not just a resource, and with the additional needs, adjustments and approaches that come with neurodivergence, investing and driving neuroinclusive cultures in conservation must become even more of a key theme for organisations than it is now. In closing this penultimate chapter, I can feel the many strands of the book beginning to weave into one. This mighty narrative thread underpins everything I've written about up until now. It's the golden one. Just what can we and are we going to do about all of this?

CHAPTER FOURTEEN
Weaving words into golden threads
Why biodiversity needs neurodiversity

Much like the neurodivergent brain, this book has been a collection of tangents. This will sound a bit weird, but the process of putting it together looks like one of those paper Chinese lanterns. It began as a narrow thematic field, funnelling out, no, exploding, into a supernova of ideas and themes, which I then had to channel into a narrative and then compact into a coherent ending. That's where we are now. Throughout our education, we are taught that a story must have a beginning, a middle and an end for it to flow in a way that we can process. Weaving multiple strands together, when your brain would rather send them off in different directions, is a challenging task. I feel like the authorial equivalent of the Miller's daughter in Rumpelstiltskin. Except I'm weaving words into golden threads, not straw. As much as I'm working with solid themes, neurodivergence and conservation, the most fascinating element of all of this, for me, has been the writing process, or the lack of one. Finality is not a construct that comes easy to me, as with many others with ADHD. We may be abstract thinkers, but finishing any task can feel like an impossibility.

Therefore, drawing this book to a close has been striking fear into me for most of the two-and-a-half years that I've been writing it. The fluid nature of the book has meant that at times I haven't been able to comprehend when and how it could end, and I suppose if I'm honest, part of me doesn't want it to. I know that this is because it'll leave a massive hole, where it's been dominating my life for so long, but also because both the natural world and neurodivergence are gifts that just keep on giving. There's still so much to explore about the intersection of the two. I can remember the specific moment when it all became coherent. Şeniz Mustafa and I were chatting, and she threw me a curveball, asking if I thought that most of the people in the conservation sector were neurodivergent, whether they knew it or not. She had been having conversations about it for a while, and even her lecturers had jokingly said that half the students on her course have learning support plans in place. She feels like she just clicks with most people she speaks to in the sector, and wonders if it's because they're also neurodivergent.

It's a topic that has come up in several of the interviews for this book, and in general chats with the contributors. Most of the people I spoke to feel that there's an above-average representation of neurodivergent people in the conservation sector, and they work with them at all levels, from the boardroom to the boardwalk. We know that specific data on this isn't on the EDI agenda (yet), and therefore annual reporting doesn't and isn't going to reflect the true numbers. I can't help but think that neurodivergent people are drawn towards the conservation sector for the same unifying reasons and purposes. We just want to conserve the entity that understands us, that makes us feel safe, and gives us the escape we crave. We also desperately want to impart that desire to protect it to other people, but for so many of us, communication just isn't a strong point. It's not a coincidence that we'd rather spend our time with the thing that we most want to keep safe, than the people who wreak havoc upon it. However, the paradox is that we need to engage these people, and change their perceptions and attitudes, to stand any chance of making positive change happen.

My own perspective on neurodivergence shifts all the time. Some days, I'll be loving the concept of being neurodivergent. I'll be exercising the adjustments and employment protections that can come with it, discussing my own experiences to support other people, embracing my differences, and even finding myself writing a book all about it. On another day, I experience shame and embarrassment about it. This might be due to stigma, or something in the mass media, or it might be this niggling feeling I occasionally get, when I feel that people are trivialising certain neurodivergent traits, mostly through social media. One of my original interview questions was to ask what people thought about the 'growing neurodiversity movement', and I feel it's pertinent to share some of the perspectives here. The prevailing feeling is that the modern open dialogue around neurodivergence has sent it into the forefront of people's thoughts, which has then put it on the organisational agenda, in terms of EDI.

This societal shift is seen as fantastic by most, but several people have given it some much deeper thought and argue that we must exercise far more nuance than we do. A quote given to me a few times is that 'Once you've met one neurodivergent person, that's just it, you've met one neurodivergent person'; or as another person so succinctly put it, 'We love boxes, but not everyone can be put in one.' The fact that I'm even using the word 'neurodivergent', let alone writing a book about it, shows just how far the evolution of language around individual differences has come. However, in one of our conversations, Alister Harman said that on gaming forums, he regularly experiences discriminatory language, mostly around autism. It's always lurking. We've seen from several of the employment experiences in this book that there's still a long way to go to embed truly neuroinclusive cultures, and eradicate stigma and Jurassic opinions, which were never acceptable anyway. The fact that people still balk at disclosing their neurodivergence at work corroborates this, but cultures can change. You may recall that in Chapter 2, I wrote about an anonymous member of RSPB staff and their reasons for not disclosing their autism diagnosis.

Well, that person is Emma Marsh, who happens to be an executive director of the RSPB. Shortly before finishing this book, she got in touch and said that she'd 'come out' as autistic in a blog post and described the reaction as 'amazing'. A colleague was keen to add their perspective to this and said that Emma sharing her autism diagnosis had been helpful on a personal level, teaching them that it's fine to be grappling personal challenges alongside work, and that despite barriers, you can still perform your role. It was also a robust reminder to ask for support if you need it. Emma's vulnerability is another example of a senior leader modelling inclusive practice, much like Hazel Jackson at the Woodland Trust, and it lets her colleagues know that sharing things like this is a safe thing to do. She also told them how she's using her experiences to shape internal policies and processes, demonstrating real action and leadership. In sharing her specific needs, Emma gave her colleagues the tools to be able to understand and support her better, which helps everyone. This cultural shift, over the timeline of writing the book, is a beautiful thing. It truly validates the importance of neuroinclusion and visible neurodivergence at the summit of organisations.

In contrast to Emma waiving her anonymity, several people in this book, who had been happy to share their full names alongside their opinions and experiences, had a change of heart close to submission. Thankfully for me, it's not difficult to take a name out and remove any signifiers of someone's identity, so I just did it. Each of them was keen to explain why they had chosen to do this, and it came down to preserving their reputation. However, when Emma got in touch, I found myself reflecting on whether there was an element of stigma behind these changes of heart as well. For example, someone gave strong opinions about their treatment as an employee with ADHD, and what they did to challenge this. Then they read what I wrote, which was largely verbatim, thought about it, and found themselves sinking into a negative thought spiral about coming across as righteous, impulsive and reactionary. This was a trigger for RSD and led to extensive rumination on the possible effect this might have on their future employment prospects. You can see why someone might change their mind and ask me to remove certain anecdotes, but it's a shame that these perspectives still pervade the overall thinking around neurodivergence.

This is such a good example of how neurodivergent traits can impact our thought processes. Difficulties with emotional regulation, RSD and impulsivity have led to several people oversharing with me during their interviews, and then wanting to backtrack or amend what they said. Translate this into a workplace, and it's a recipe for tension and conflict. In Chapter 7, when discussing the notion of neurodivergent strengths, I wrote about my own neurodivergence not being a superpower, and being the opposite for those people close to me. For all the wonderful aptitudes and unique skills that neurodivergent conservationists bring to their roles, we mustn't lose sight of the barriers, and negative impacts, that their conditions can cause. We might think laterally, but we can also think very literally. We may think outside the box, but we've spent a lot of our lives inside one. We might be able to hyperfocus, but we can also hyper fixate. Our senses may be sharp, but they can often be too sharp, to the point of overwhelm. We might be amazing at analysing data, but if you don't understand my spreadsheet, you're an idiot. I could go on, but hopefully you get my point.

I keep forgetting the other concurrent narrative here – you know, the other core theme of the book, the conservation sector. Mention conservation work in the UK, and it conjures up imagery of David Attenborough in the Rwandan jungle with a family of gorillas. However, we know that this isn't the reality for most conservation careers, with many people unable to get a foothold in the sector due to the barriers I've written about. A lot of work is happening to try and address these inequalities, and the faces of conservation are slowly changing to better represent our diverse society. We are starting to see improvements in gender representation and ethnic diversity in conservation, but reforming the sector to become genuinely inclusive is going to be a drawn-out process, which will probably go on for many decades. But representation is improving. One of the most recognisable people in the UK conservation media is Chris Packham, who is open about being autistic, as is the multi-award-winning nature writer, Dara McAnulty. And on a global scale, most of us are aware of Greta Thunberg, the autistic climate change activist from Sweden.

What else can we do? In Chapter 8 I wrote about the distinct lack of careers guidance for the conservation sector, but Şeniz says that the disparity traces back even further. I know full well that ecology just isn't part of the secondary school lexicon, and she says the representation of ecology in her biology A-level were some quadrats containing literally three daisies. The assumption was always that her chosen career path would result in her working in a zoo, and that would be it. The understanding of ecological processes just wasn't there, and sometimes Şeniz isn't even sure how her interest came about. Especially as she grew up in south-east London, where access to green spaces was at a premium. But she could never understand why they weren't taught about the environment in more depth at her school, particularly as it had a pond and resident geese on its grounds. It strikes me that we hear so much about the lack of access to green space, but sometimes, even when it's there, people just don't know what to do with it. We need positive role modelling more than ever.

Şeniz shares how she took her two younger cousins to visit a few local nature sites when they came to visit her, and didn't force them, but just let them take an organic interest in the wildlife. She did this to give them the opportunities to access nature that she didn't have. However, she reflects that if they didn't have her in their family, they wouldn't be engaging with nature at all, and that's the norm for so many of our young people now. Şeniz muses that it would be amazing if schools brought people in to talk to their students about careers in the conservation sector, but not to just stand at a stall, as she did this once and no one came over to engage with her. I've written about using practical and engaging approaches to try and ignite an interest in nature, and for those of us who have the privilege of working with young people and love the outdoors, using your passion to enthuse others can be one of the simplest but most effective tools in your kit. Nature is as cool as you make it, and if you love it, let that love shine through.

Şeniz is like so many other people, and just prefers doing hands-on things outdoors. She wonders if this is a trait of neurodivergence, and after speaking to so many neurodivergent conservationists, I recognise that there may well be a correlation there. She uses an example of the irony in doing an online class about bird identification, when there's no better way to hone these skills than to spend time in the field, in what I would describe as full sensory immersion. I completely agree that there's no substitute for experiential nature connection and learning. She says it's similar when she's in a lecture, and unless the content is genuinely engaging or the lecturer is a big character, her brain eventually switches off as it's just not stimulating enough for her. Her concentration is infinitely better outside, and I can relate to this a lot. However, I do think this is contextual. I wouldn't be able to perform the office elements of my role whilst outdoors, as the sounds and visuals of nature would constantly divert my attention. We both agree that the perfect combination is a balance of well-thought-out lecture-type activities with practical and vocational experiences. Apprenticeships, anyone?

I had already thought to laud the benefits of the apprenticeship in this book, especially after writing so much about alternative approaches to learning for neurodivergent people. How serendipitous then, that just before submitting the book manuscript, I read an article saying that the Chartered Institute of Ecology and Environmental Management (CIEEM) have just been given the green light by a regulatory body, to develop a full proposal for a Level-4 ecology apprenticeship. The CIEEM are trailblazers in shaping the sector for the future, and as well as Lea Nightingale leading on EDI, Brian Heppenstall has left his teaching job and now works for them, leading on education and careers. One of their recent initiatives is Green Jobs for Nature, a hub of realistic information, advice and guidance for anyone looking at working in a green industry. Their website outlines various roles, sectors and pathways, and provides research, case studies and guest blogs to supplement this. It feels current and accessible, using simple but effective presentation of information. I particularly like their jargon buster, and their list of tips on good working practice. The site really feels like it has been put together by people who understand how difficult it can be to seek out roles in the sector and want to support others through this.

Ecologist Larissa Cooper makes a great suggestion of something we could do differently. She says that there are many routes into working in ecology, and going from further to higher education seems to be the industry expectation. Yes, the sector is competitive, but if you're someone with good knowledge of a specific taxonomic group, she says there'll always be work as identification is incredibly important. What she'd like to see are apprenticeships, with the option to upskill at degree-level. I also couldn't agree more with her next point that neurodivergent people often struggle with school and burn out in further education, if they even make it that far. As she says, how amazing would it be if they could get an apprenticeship, learn ecology on the job and then consolidate this into a degree later if necessary for progression? Speaking from experience, she adds that most ecology degrees focus on research and end up overpreparing students for the sector. I have always been a supporter of vocational learning pathways, and the idea of staggering the heavy academia like this is responsive, bespoke and inclusive. I love it.

Dr Steve Allain also feels strongly about the higher-education system, and as he's a university lecturer, he's going to have a particularly relevant insight into the matter. What he does is suggest a series of practical adjustments that could be put in place for neurodivergent students at all levels. He says that there should always be the option for part-time study (look at the success of working from home, post-Covid), flexible deadlines and asynchronous learning to better support the processing of information. Async, what? It means having access to course materials at any time, to learn whenever, and usually doesn't feature 'live' teaching. He also thinks that we should offer and use a variety of assessment methods, as exam conditions don't work for everyone. My experience bears this out; even with adjustments in place for exams (access arrangements), I've still seen neurodivergent children crumble under the pressure. There are many alternative frameworks for the assessment of learning, which allow the demonstration of knowledge in ways that respect individual differences. Steve also questions why so many adjustments are seemingly exclusive for those with a diagnosis. We both know it's a systemic funding issue.

One thing that Steve, coastal consultant Emily Clarke and I all agree on is that there should be much more consideration given to the physical spaces that we work and learn in. Not enough workplaces and academic settings provide sensory-friendly spaces, such as quiet zones and sensory rooms, for people to take breaks in a low-stimulation environment. As Emily says, this can't be a spare room off a kitchen or walkway, it needs to be somewhere that's away from the workplace. Think back to the requisites for a restorative environment, and one of them is to be 'away'. It also can't be a space where someone 'just makes a phone call' or 'holds a quick one-to-one as all the meeting rooms are in use' – it just defeats the point of having the space in the first place. Emily says that conference organisers need to ensure that these spaces are available and advertise them, and why shouldn't conference and event venues offer this as a standard, anyway? This would reduce the cost of having to hire an extra room, which is what usually ends up happening. Ultimately, it's best practice, as we know from the National Trust's Workability Conference.

I know that in Chapter 11 I got a bit giddy about the use of infographics, but all flippancy aside, the way that we share and condense information about the environment should be an integral consideration for all who work in the sector. The key role of conservation communicators was a feature of Chapter 5, but what's just as significant as the messenger, is the message. Reducing technical language, and using clear and unambiguous wording, must be the gold standard. In terms of the delivery, the way that we distil key messages is vital. A lot of the people I spoke to felt that the sector was a bit 'stale', especially through the lens of diversity, and using engaging communication is a crucial way of combating this. I wrote earlier about engaging hard-to-reach groups through showing them that there are faces and voices they can relate to. I believe this to be the strongest tool we have at our disposal, and some of the prominent 'sci-comms' people on social media are leading the way in how to do this effectively. We must be careful that this doesn't become a form of tokenism though, and diverse voices don't become a commodification.

New initiatives for engaging young people with nature are thankfully appearing all the time, such as 'Generation Nature'. The young people leading this project got in touch with me, ironically, through social media, and I simply had to include them. Generation Nature are a collective of young people working on the creation of an entirely youth-led podcast made exclusively for young people. It focusses on storytelling for nature, with the aim of showcasing a diverse range of stories from young people. They hope that this will facilitate empathetic and inquisitive responses from their target audience, while demonstrating that the natural world is for everyone, and therefore we must all fight to conserve it. From their own experiences, and those they witness every day, the team behind it know that a disconnect from nature often manifests during the teenage years. They believe that storytelling is one of the most powerful and effective ways of reaching young people. This is because they think it brings an emotional resonance that simply regurgitating facts and figures doesn't achieve. Their stories will emerge from their own positions of experience and empathy, alongside exploring and tackling the common barriers young people face when trying to engage with nature.

It came about after the group met on another project, Young Voices for Nature, which was a collaboration between the RSPB, the National Trust and the World Wildlife Fund's UK arm. How refreshingly positive to see two of the NGOs from Chapter 10 walking the walk when it comes to youth engagement, as part of the Save Our Wild Isles campaign. The Young Voices for Nature project is worth having a look at, especially the youth-led film that was made as a result. The crux of the project was creative storytelling, and the group had such a positive experience that they kept in touch afterwards. This is what eventually led to the creation of Generation Nature, which they want to be entirely driven by young people, in all aspects. I ask them what involvement neurodivergent young people have in the project, and they say that they are a neurodiverse team working on the podcast. Their individual perspectives make the project both highly collaborative and diverse, each bringing different skills to what they're working on. As well as having an aim, they are also friends, and strongly feel that the friendly, enjoyable and informal way that they work is conducive to an inclusive environment. I can't say that I disagree with them.

Generation Nature sounds like it's going to be an insightful and engaging resource, but I love how even though it's being made for an external audience, it has had myriad internal benefits for its team, too. Particularly one of them, James, who has such a profundity in his experiences that it compels me to include them. James is both autistic and a young carer, which together must create significant barriers to, well, everything. He describes finding 'so much joy in our natural world, the rustle of the leaves, the flowers growing between the pavement and the road, and the community.' But it's hard for James to find the time for nature connection, and his main opportunity is his 25-minute walk to school through suburban habitats. Along the journey, every day, he writes poetry about nature on his phone, and how its loss makes him feel. He admits that he's often the target of teasing from other young people who don't understand why he points out and takes photos of nature. I've seen firsthand a feeling amongst young people that having an interest in nature is 'uncool', so uniting with people who share that love can help counter any feelings of isolation.

A lot of people had concerns about how difficult it is to access assessments for diagnoses, with the consensus being that we need a radical systemic overhaul. I don't know what the answer is, and there are so many conflicting suggestions out there, that I'm going to avoid trying to deconstruct it here. Increasing awareness is the golden bullet for effecting cultural change at every level, but I can't help wondering what might happen to the already-broken system if the rate of diagnosis continues on such a steep upward trend. I suppose we risk overwhelming and crashing some of the systems of support we have in place, such as Access to Work and pharmaceutical prescription medication. However, it could end up making reasonable adjustments, and accepting individual ways of working, a standard part of working life. It reminds me of how the Environment Agency are rolling out their workplace passports to all their staff, which is incredible, but imagine if we got to a position where celebrating difference was simply part of our culture and systems. For now, I applaud those conservation organisations that are embracing reasonable adjustments creatively and effectively, lighting the way for others to follow suit.

I haven't written much about the need for interview adjustments as part of the recruitment process, mainly because it's far from unique to the sector, and has been a prominent theme of discussions about neurodivergence at work for a while now. Many of the people I spoke to, both individuals and organisations, felt that standard interview procedures should be, in Lottie Trewick's words, 'thrown out of the window'. So many interview approaches, whatever format they take, bring their own unique barriers for neurodivergent applicants. To be honest, I find that filling in a job application form requires a monumental level of concentration, and I often give up way before completing them. There are lots of tweaks we can make, and the one that most people mention is to request interview questions in advance so they can prepare effectively, and not freeze when put on the spot, or give a short, anxiety-driven response. These are just a few examples of reactions in formal interviews. Lottie makes a great suggestion: that employers could offer an informal conversation, either in person or over the phone, as part of the interview process. This might reduce the pressure of social expectations and conventions, perhaps helping someone to express themselves in their 'usual' manner.

This 'usual manner' is part of the fundamental beauty of neurodiversity. Throughout this book are some stellar examples of how neurodivergent conservationists have been harnessing their differences and strengths to push towards a common goal of conserving the environment. Take a moment to rejoice in COP28, the Seychelles' black parrots, astronomical apple seeds, white stork pellets, pine marten recovery, and bareroot tree growing. Now that's a sentence absolutely thriving with diversity if ever I saw one. However, if we take a step back and gain a wider perspective, we can see that the reality of neurodivergence in the conservation sector is far from ideal. Approaches to neuroinclusion across the sector are fragmentary at best, with some areas of outstanding practice, and some terrible tales of discrimination and needs not being met. As I said earlier, I could have chosen to just share the negative responses, but that would only perpetuate a negative cycle. I stand by my assertion that partnership working and sharing best practice are both imperative for progressing the inclusive culture of the sector. We don't need to standardise, just share more, as retaining our individual differences, whether personally or organisationally, is the fundamental ethos of neurodiversity, isn't it?

We are currently standing on an environmental precipice. Our population is growing whilst space to live is diminishing. Habitats are disappearing as our climate is changing beyond recognition. To combat these challenges, we need diverse perspectives, innovative ideas and radical approaches. We need neurodivergence. We need it where it matters, whether that's knee-deep in the meadows surveying insects, or sitting round a table deciding the next year's strategic objectives for an NGO. To ensure our planet has a resilient and hopeful future, we must embrace and promote all forms of diversity. A diverse future is a flourishing one, and to secure this for the next generations and beyond, we must all commit to inclusivity. Our structures and processes need to adapt and adjust to nurture neurodivergence, and I mean this generally, not just in the conservation sector. There is an obvious intersection of all the barriers and challenges in this book, and a systemic shift toward a genuinely inclusive culture will be the only way we can tackle them. The future of conservation isn't just about protecting the world around us, it's also about ensuring that everyone gets the opportunity to play their part in doing so. That's why biodiversity needs neurodiversity.

Acknowledgements

Thanks to the diverse range of people who I spoke to for this book, particularly those I've stayed in contact with. Barbara, Colin, Hazel, Emily, Alister, Tracey, Lucy Mo, Lottie, James H, Alex, Michael, Alice, Larissa, Helen, Mark, Naomi, Steve, Şeniz, Steph, Lucy Mc, Adam, Kerryn, Joe B, Pete, Eddie, Thom, Inez, Brian, Georgina, Mya, Andrew, Ajay, Aisha, Lea, Simon, Vera, Lavinia, Paul, James D, Sophie, Mikael, Wali, Lauren, Matt, Gill, Joe NM, Kit, Cate, Tom, Chris, Lou, Emma, Ellen, Emma M, Raman, Freddie, and James D.

To my wife for accepting and understanding that this was a book worth writing and allowing me to do so; to my daughters, for being themselves and grounding me; to my grandparents, who remain such an inspirational force in my life.

To the team at Bloomsbury for deciding to take on this book and making no end of adjustments to accommodate my neurodivergence – my editors, Julie and Amy; my marketer, Sarah; and my cover designer, Lora. To Ruth, my publicist, again, accommodating me and accepting my limitations.

To Elizabeth and Jo, for their thorough copy-edit and proofread, respectively, that gave the text the final uplift it needed; to Lauren, for creating the gorgeous cover art and to Paul, Kelly, and Group B, for helping me to choose the final version; to Jon and Sacha, for their unwavering support and humour, always; and to Dave, for the message that started it all.

To Liam and Jonathan, for the Banter Bus; to my old school for being flexible and allowing me some time off to interview people; to methylphenidate, for helping me to be able to focus on writing; and finally, to everyone who was negative about my first book – because of you all, I'm a better writer.

Further reading and resources

General resources

The UK Equality Act (2010): gov.uk/definition-of-disability-under-equality-act-2010
DSM-5: psychiatry.org/psychiatrists/practice/dsm
Education Health and Care Plans: gov.uk/children-with-special-educational-needs/extra-SEN-help

Neurodivergent conditions covered in this book

For more information about specific neurodivergent diagnoses, there is plenty of accessible information available via the NHS, neurodivergent charities and related organisations.

ADHD UK: adhduk.co.uk
ADHD in adults, NHS: nhs.uk/conditions/adhd-adults
ADHD in young people, NHS: nhs.uk/conditions/adhd-children-teenagers
ADHD and driving, licencing and the DVLA: gov.uk/adhd-and-driving

National Autistic Society (NAS): autism.org.uk
Autism, NHS: nhs.uk/conditions/autism
Autism Education Trust: autismeducationtrust.org.uk
'Failing a generation' report: bma.org.uk/media/2056/autism-briefing.pdf
NAS outline of an ADOD assessment: autism.org.uk/advice-and-guidance/topics/diagnosis/assessment-and-diagnosis/criteria-and-tools-used-in-an-autism-assessment
NAS focused and dedicated interests: autism.org.uk/advice-and-guidance/topics/about-autism/focused-and-dedicated-interests

The British Dyslexia Association, Dyslexia: bdadyslexia.org.uk
Dyscalculia: bdadyslexia.org.uk/dyscalculia
Dyspraxia: bdadyslexia.org.uk/dyslexia/neurodiversity-and-co-occurring-differences/dyspraxia
Dysgraphia, ADDitude article: additudemag.com/what-is-dysgraphia-understanding-common-symptoms

FURTHER READING AND RESOURCES

Nature-based forms of education

Edfords Care Farm: edfordscarefarm.co.uk
Social Farms and Gardens: farmgarden.org.uk
Steiner Waldorf Education: waldorfeducation.uk
The Wilderness Grove: thewildernessgrove.co.uk

Inclusivity in workplaces and organisations

CIPD website, to find out more about neuroinclusive workplaces: cipd.org/uk/topics/equality-diversity-inclusion
Countryside Jobs Service, Alister Harman: news.countryside-jobs.com/2022/05/conservation-neurodivergent-me.html
Countryside Jobs Service, Brian Heppenstall: countryside-jobs.com/article/2019-09-04-conservation-an-accessible-industry
Journalism Diversity Fund: nctj.com/journalism-diversity-fund
Joint Nature Conservation Committee: jncc.gov.uk
Racial Action for the Climate Emergency: race-report.uk

Conservation organisations, NGOs and projects mentioned in this book

Bat Conservation Trust (BCT): bats.org.uk
The Blandford Fly: fantasticpestcontrol.co.uk/flies/the-blandford-fly
Bright Green Business: brightgreenbusiness.org.uk
British Dragonfly Society: british-dragonflies.org.uk
British Trust for Ornithology (BTO): bto.org
Bumblebee Conservation Trust: bumblebeeconservation.org
Butterfly Conservation: butterfly-conservation.org
Cameron Bespolka Trust: cameronbespolka.com
Chartered Institute of Ecology and Environmental Management (CIEEM): cieem.net
COP26: un.org/en/climatechange/cop26
COP28: unfccc.int/cop28/5-key-takeaways and Mangrove Restoration work: cop28.com/en/nature-events/mangrove-ministerial
Countryside Jobs Service: countryside-jobs.com
Environment Agency: gov.uk/government/organisations/environment-agency
Forestry Commission: gov.uk/government/organisations/forestry-commission

Generation Nature: generationnature.org.uk
Green Jobs for Nature: greenjobsfornature.org
The Grower: thegrower.co.uk
Hazel Jackson, Seychelles Black Parrot: bou.org.uk/blog-jackson-black-parrot
Knepp Estate: knepp.co.uk
Lyme Park, National Trust: nationaltrust.org.uk/visit/cheshire-greater-manchester/lyme
Mammal Society: mammal.org.uk
National Trust: nationaltrust.org.uk
Natural England: gov.uk/government/organisations/natural-england
NatureScot: nature.scot
Newton's Apple Seeds project: sciencecentres.org.uk/projects/newtons-apple-seeds
Pine Marten Recovery Project: ptes.org/grants/uk-mammal-projects/pine-marten-recovery-project
Plantlife International: plantlife.org.uk
Rise and Rewild: riserewild.co.uk
Royal Society for the Protection of Birds (RSPB): rspb.org.uk
RSPB Minismere Nature Reserve: rspb.org.uk/days-out/reserves/minsmere
Royal Society of Wildlife Trusts: wildlifetrusts.org
Seychelles Islands Foundation (SIF): sif.sc
St. Catherine's Hill Nature Reserve: hiwwt.org.uk/nature-reserves/st-catherines-hill-nature-reserve
Tring Natural History Museum: nhm.ac.uk/visit/tring.html
UNFCCC: unfccc.int/process-and-meetings/what-is-the-united-nations-framework-convention-on-climate-change
UK Youth for Nature (UKY4N): uky4n.org
White Stork Project: whitestorkproject.org
Wildlife and Countryside Link: wcl.org.uk
Woodland Trust: woodlandtrust.org.uk
Young Voices for Nature: saveourwildisles.org.uk/community/young-voices-for-nature

Finally, let's go back to the message that started this whole book. If you want to learn more about the incredible world of moths, the Norfolk Moths website, although county-specific, has some excellent information for beginners: norfolkmoths.co.uk

Index

Access to Work 112, 155, 176, 207, 244
achievements, career 111–27
ADHD Foundation 201
ADHD *see* attention deficit hyperactivity disorder
adult diagnosis 10, 26, 33, 34, 37, 39, 48
Allain, Steve 85–6, 104, 240
alternative provisions (APs) 213–14, 218, 220, 221
anonymity 23, 36–7, 134–5, 148, 234–5
apprenticeships 238–9
Armstrong, Alice 69, 142
ART *see* attention restoration theory
Asasumasu, Kassiane 12
ASD *see* autism spectrum disorder
attention deficit hyperactivity disorder (ADHD)
  in conservation sector 22, 32, 34, 69, 87, 90, 182
  diagnosis 9–11, 13, 27–9, 60, 147
  symptoms, traits and types 10, 14–15, 20–1, 28, 62, 94, 102, 154, 166, 174, 231
attention focus *see* hyperfocus
attention restoration theory (ART) 62
AuDHD 18
author 233
  diagnosis of ADHD 9–10, 27–9, 60, 147
  early life and educational experiences 29–30, 43–4
  nature connections 59, 62, 63–4
  reasonable adjustments in employment 147–8

  teaching experience 11, 31, 64
  see also writing process
autism spectrum disorder (ASD) 11, 13, 15–16
  in conservation sector 22, 33, 36, 48, 68, 69, 82, 87, 90, 91, 100, 101, 156, 174, 233, 236
  diagnosis 30–2, 36
  symptoms and traits 16, 94, 100–2, 111, 113
Autumnwatch 120

Bambrick, Mya 133–4, 137
Barbara 32–3
barriers
  to diagnosis 30
  to recruitment in conservation 129–44
Bat Conservation Trust (BCT) 208–10
Berkshire, Buckinghamshire and Oxfordshire Wildlife Trust 32
Binnies 22, 95, 140
Bird, William 60
BirdLife Cyprus 122
BirdLife International 89
Birmingham & Black Country Wildlife Trust 138
Bishop-Howes, Lou 221–5
block learning 56
Blume, Harvey 12
body doubling 166, 174
Bradley, Ellen 226–8
Bramwell, Lavinia 173, 175, 176
Bright Green Business 142
Bristowe, Joe 99–100
British Dragonfly Society 197–8
British Medical Association 31

British Trust for Ornithology
    (BTO)   134, 206–8
Broads Authority   180
Brown, Eddie   101–2
BTO *see* British Trust for
    Ornithology
bullying   36, 44, 45, 46, 51
Bumblebee Conservation
    Trust   204–5
Business Disability Forum   190
Butterfly Conservation   205–6
Byrne, Thom   111–15

Cameron Bespolka Trust   134
Campbell, Patrick   142
care farms   220–5
Casson, Elizabeth   71
Catalyst Science Discovery Centre
    and Museum   123
Changing Places   175
charities *see* conservation charities,
    smaller; non-governmental
    organisations *and under*
    individual charities
Chartered Institute of Ecology and
    Environmental Management
    (CIEEM)   141, 238–9
Chaudary, Mikael   189–90, 191, 192
childhood diagnosis   10, 34, 35
Churcher, Tracey   38–9, 107,
    174–5, 176
CIEEM *see* Chartered Institute of
    Ecology and Environmental
    Management
Clarke, Emily   22, 34–5, 95, 140,
    240–1
communication preferences   152
communication work   88–9; *see*
    also sci-comm
comorbidities   11, 18, 39, 60, 67
conferences   175–6, 241
Conners scales   28
conservation charities,
    smaller   197–212

Conservation Equity Project
    (CEP)   69
conservation sector   77
  ADHD in   22, 32, 34, 69, 87, 90,
    182
  autism in   22, 33, 36, 48, 68, 69,
    82, 87, 90, 91, 100, 101, 156,
    174, 233, 236
  barriers to recruitment
    129–44
  career achievements   111–27
  careers in practical
    conservation   80–4
  dyslexia in   22, 23, 34–5, 54, 71,
    87–8, 96, 99, 100, 125, 148–9,
    186
  dyspraxia in   22, 47
  ethnic diversity   138, 139, 141,
    142, 163, 172, 236
  framework   79–80
  need for neurodiversity   231–46
  pay   136–7, 142
  qualifications required   78, 85,
    129
  recruitment interviews   50, 130,
    146–7, 186, 191, 204, 244–5
  recruitment websites   50, 91,
    130, 239
  volunteer work   78, 87, 101, 107,
    118, 120, 122, 129, 130, 135,
    136, 137, 139, 141, 142, 167,
    168, 172
  youth engagement   85, 134, 200,
    226–8, 241–3
Cooper, Larissa   69, 70, 81–2, 97,
    104, 239
coping   15, 36, 39, 67, 103
Countryside Agency   181
Countryside Jobs Service   50, 91,
    130
Covid pandemic   30, 73, 97,
    112, 151, 153, 166, 192, 240
creativity   56, 88, 93, 96, 153, 219,
    226–7

INDEX

Davis, Naomi 82–3, 97–8, 103–4, 118–20
DEI *see* equality, diversity and inclusion
Department for Environment, Food and Rural Affairs (Defra) 112, 180, 181, 183, 193
Department for Work and Pensions (DWP) 155, 156
diagnosis
  ADHD 10–11
  adult 10, 26, 33, 34, 37, 39, 48
  autism 30–2, 36
  barriers to 30
  benefits of 25–6, 33, 40
  childhood 10, 34, 35
  disclosure reluctance 26, 37, 61, 234
  dual 11
  girls and women 15, 16
  private 27, 32, 35
  subjectivity 26–7
  upward trend 244
  waiting times 28, 32
Diamond, James 183–5
directed attention fatigue (DAF) 62, 63
Disability Discrimination Act 145
disclosure 145, 147, 184, 234–5
disclosure reluctance 26, 37, 61, 234
discriminatory language 33, 39, 49, 233
Driver and Vehicle Licensing Agency (DVLA) 29
dyscalculia 13, 17, 18
dysgraphia 13, 17, 18
dyslexia 13, 17, 22, 23, 34–5, 54, 71, 87–8, 96, 99, 100, 125, 148–9, 155, 186
dyspraxia 13, 17, 22, 47, 191

Edfords Care Farm 221–5
EDI *see* equality, diversity and inclusion

education, environmental 84–5, 236–7
education, experiences in 43–58
  author's 29–30, 43–4
  culture and inflexibility 43, 57–8, 66, 220
  exclusion and non-attendance 44–5, 57, 67
  higher education 54, 240
  primary schools 43, 45, 49, 71
  private schools 35, 49–50
  secondary schools 29, 35, 44, 45, 49, 51, 213, 236
  see also care farms; exams; forest schools; homeschooling *and* Steiner schools
education, health and care plans (EHCPs) 26, 47, 150
empathy 95, 100–1, 102, 105, 107, 159, 216, 242
enhanced pattern recognition 100
Environment Agency 156, 179, 187–92, 244
environmental education 84–5, 236–7
Equality Act 26, 145, 179–80
equality, diversity and inclusion (EDI) 91, 138, 139, 141
  in government agencies 179–95
  in non-governmental organisations 161–77
  in smaller conservation charities 197–212
Ethan 224–5
ethnic diversity in conservation 138, 139, 141, 142, 163, 172, 236
Everett, Colin 22, 33–4, 48–50, 83–4, 97
exams 17, 54, 58, 62, 213, 240

farms 56, 104–5; *see also* care farms
fidget toys 154, 174, 175
flexible working 151–2, 153, 169, 174, 192

Floyd, George   192
forest schools   214–20
Forestry Commission   180, 193–5

Generation Nature   241–3
girls and women, under-diagnosis in   15, 16
global population, neurodivergence in   13
government agencies and departments   112, 155, 156, 179–95
Green Jobs for Nature   239
grounding   69
The Grower   124, 125
Gupwell, Matt   204, 205
Gwent Wildlife Trust   90

Hampshire Wildlife Trust   52
handwriting difficulties   18
Hankins, James   22, 55–6, 104–5, 153–4
Harding, Alex   66, 221
Harman, Alister   38, 50–1, 65, 66, 80–1, 96, 98–9, 105–6, 122–3, 157, 174, 233
hearing   45, 97, 224
Heppenstall, Brian   129–31, 238
Hill, Octavia   176
Hinds, Paul   182–3, 185
homeschooling   47, 217, 225
Howard, Michael   68, 69, 174
Howes, Chris   221–5
human relationships, difficulties with   39, 101
Humphreys, Kerryn   91–2
hyperesthesia   98
hyperfocus   94, 96–7, 102, 105, 117, 122, 198, 236

inclusive practices *see* neuroinclusion
infographics   13, 189, 193, 241
interviews
    recruitment   50, 130, 146–7, 186, 191, 204, 244–5

and writing process   19–20, 22, 53, 154, 189, 232, 233

Jackson, Hazel   22, 34, 94–5, 115–17, 152–3, 154, 198–200, 234
James   243
jobs in conservation *see* conservation sector
Joint Nature Conservation Committee (JNCC)   79
Journalism Diversity Fund   88
justice, sense of   105, 106

Kaplan, Rachel and Stephen   62–3
Kennedy, Lauren   197–8
Kew Gardens *see* Royal Botanic Gardens Kew
Knepp Estate   121

Lantra   141
Larsen-Daw, Matt   201–4
leaders, neurodivergent   37, 90–1, 95, 158, 169, 171, 176, 200, 234
legislation   26, 145, 179–80, 181
Lexxic   141
literacy skills   17

Mahmood, Aisha   138–40
Mammal Society   201–4
Marsh, Emma   234
Martin, Stephanie   87–8
masking   16, 32, 36, 67, 107, 118, 119, 151, 157
Mason, Helen   70–4
Mayhew, Georgina   131–2
McAnulty, Dara   236
McRobert, Lucy   88–90
meltdown   16, 62, 65, 107
memory skills   94
mental health   15, 32, 39, 46, 59, 60, 67, 70, 72, 120, 168, 175, 206, 224
Morris, Lucy   22, 45–8, 151

INDEX

moths, interest in 7–9, 19, 67
motor skills 17
Mustafa, Şeniz 86–7, 105, 106–7, 121–2, 137, 143, 232, 236–8

National Autistic Society (NAS) 15, 32, 102
National Health Service (NHS) 10, 15, 27, 28, 30, 31–2, 70
National Park authorities 130, 180
National Trust 38, 68, 80, 107, 136, 157, 172–7, 241, 242
Natural England 79, 124, 179, 181–7
Natural Environment Investment Readiness Fund 114
Natural History Museum 115, 142
nature connections, benefits of 59–75
networks, staff diversity 156, 158, 168–9, 173, 179, 183–4, 189–92, 193–4
neurodevelopmental disorders 10–11
neurodiversity, term 12
neuroinclusion 106, 203–4, 210, 234, 245–6
neurotypicality 13
NGOs *see* non-governmental organisations
niche obsessions 7–9, 19; *see also* special interests
Nightingale, Lea 141, 238
noise sensitivity 65, 68, 97–8
non-governmental organisations (NGOs) 161–77
non-judgemental environments 65, 66, 67, 74, 220, 221
Norfolk Wildlife Trust 84, 167
Not so Freshwater campaign 226, 227
numbers, difficulties with 17–18, 45
Nunez-Mino, Joe 208, 209, 210

occupational therapy 71–2
outdoor learning 66, 213–14, 225–7; *see also* care farms *and* forest schools

pay in conservation sector 136–7, 142
Peake, Tim 123
Perkins, Gill 204–5
Pine Marten Recovery Project 118
Pips in Space project 123
Plantlife International 89, 201
private diagnosis 27, 32, 35
problem-solving 65, 93, 94, 125, 221
proprioception 72, 219
Public Sector Equality Duty 179–80
public speaking 106–7
Pudilova, Vera 156–7, 190

qualifications required in conservation 78, 85, 129
quiet spaces 147, 175, 194, 240

Racial Action for the Climate Emergency (RACE) 135, 137, 138
Rahman, Wali 193, 194
reasonable adjustments 145–60, 164–6
recruitment
  barriers to 129–44
  websites 50, 91, 130, 239
  see also interviews: recruitment
Regi, Cate 215–20, 225
rejection sensitive dysphoria (RSD) 174, 235
repetitive behaviours 16, 102
Rise and Rewild 70, 73–4
risk-taking 14, 39, 117, 215
Ritchie, Karen 142
Rivers Trust 227

Royal Botanic Gardens Kew 123, 180
Royal Society for the Protection of Birds (RSPB) 36, 37, 80, 136, 154, 156, 163–7, 183, 234, 242, 234

safe spaces 62, 64
Save Our Wild Isles campaign 242
schools *see* education, experiences in
sci-comm (science-communication) 87–90, 241
SEND *see* special educational needs and disabilities
sensory processing disorders 16, 49, 65, 98
Seychelles Islands Foundation 116
shutdown 16, 46, 63, 65, 107
siblings, neurodivergence in 38–9
Singer, Judy 12
sit spots 68
Smith, Heather 173, 175
Social Farms and Gardens 221
Sound Approach 89
special educational needs and disabilities (SEND) 32, 54, 66, 214, 216
special interests 94, 102–5, 198; *see also* niche obsessions
specific learning disorders (SpLDs) 11, 16–18, 67, 94
Springwatch 133
Steiner schools 55–6
Stennet, Simon 154–5, 164–7
stigma 12, 34, 36, 37, 40, 61, 108, 169, 233, 234, 235
stimming 16
Stoner, Kit 210
strengths and skills of neurodivergent people 93–109

Taylor, Adam 90–1
Tegala, Ajay 137, 138, 140
toilets, accessible 175

Tomlin, Pete 100, 106
training, staff diversity 159, 171, 185, 190, 191, 193, 194, 200, 201, 205
Trewick, Lottie 22, 52, 53–4, 95–6, 244
Tumber, Sophie 189

UK Youth for Nature (UKY₄N) 226–8
urban settings 61–2, 69

Valencia, Lira 85
visual-spatial sense 99–100
volunteer work in conservation 78, 87, 101, 107, 118, 120, 122, 129, 130, 135, 136, 137, 139, 141, 142, 167, 168, 172

Watkins, Kenneth 199
Whitelee, Andrew 135–7
Wild, Tom 215, 218–19, 220, 225
Wilderness Grove Forest School 215–220, 225
Wildlife and Countryside Link 141, 208, 227
Wildlife Trusts 32, 52, 84, 89, 90, 100, 138, 167–72
Williams-Green, Tyler 142
Williams-King, Inez 124–6, 186
Woodland Trust 22, 94, 115, 153, 199–201
WorkAbility conferences 175–6
workplace passports 148, 156, 157, 165, 169, 185, 192, 194, 199, 244
writing process 19–20, 22, 53, 154, 189, 231–2, 233
WWF-UK 242

Young Voices for Nature 242
Your Wild Streets campaign 227
youth engagement 85, 134, 200, 226–8, 241–3